beyond black

BIRACIAL IDENTITY
IN AMERICA

KERRY ANN ROCKQUEMORE
Boston College

DAVID L. BRUNSMA
University of Alabama, Huntsville

Sage Publications
International Educational and Professional Publisher
Thousand Oaks ▪ London ▪ New Delhi

For information:

Sage Publications, Inc.
2455 Teller Road
Thousand Oaks, California 91320
E-mail: order@sagepub.com

Sage Publications Ltd.
6 Bonhill Street
London EC2A 4PU
United Kingdom

Sage Publications India Pvt. Ltd.
M-32 Market
Greater Kailash I
New Delhi 110 048 India

Printed in the United States of America

Library of Congress Cataloging-in-Publication Data

Rockquemore, Kerry.
   Beyond Black: Biracial identity in America / by Kerry Ann Rockquemore and David L. Brunsma.
      p. cm.
   Includes bibliographical references and index.
   ISBN 0-7619-2322-5 (pbk.)
   1. Racially mixed people—United States—Race identity. 2. Racially mixed people—United States—Psychology. 3. Racially mixed people—United States—Social conditions. 4. United States—Race relations. 5. United States—Race relations—Psychological aspects. 6. United States—Race relations—Statistics. 7. Social surveys—United States. I. Brunsma, David L. II. Title.
   E184.A1 R62 2001
   305.8'00973—dc21   2001001391

This book is printed on acid-free paper.

   03   04   05   06   7   6   5   4   3

Acquiring Editor: Jim Brace-Thompson
Editorial Assistant: Karen Ehrmann
Production Editor: Sanford Robinson
Editorial Assistant: Ester Marcelino
Typesetter: Denyse Dunn
Indexer: Molly Hall
Cover Designer: Ravi Balasuriya

Contents

To

William and Rachel

Preface

In 1997, the Office of Management and Budget announced that a multi-racial category would not be added to the 2000 census. This decision followed a protracted and heated debate among multiracial activists, parents of biracial children, statisticians, politicians, academics, civil rights organizations, and various interest groups about the necessity and propriety of adding a new racial category. The debate that had occurred, both in the legislative arena and in the popular press, was dominated by emotional rhetoric. Little empirical evidence existed about the way that multiracial people understand their racial identities. In fact, the Census 2000 Advisory Committee was given Maria Root's anthology, *Racially Mixed People in America,* as mandatory reading because it was, at the time, considered the most cutting-edge research on the multiracial population. This cutting-edge research, however, included chapters written by multiracial activists and leaders of multiracial organizations (such as AMEA and I-Pride) and, in its one-sided support of the multiracial category, was devoid of critical analysis of the multiracial movement. In addition, the text was heavy with conceptual and theoretical essays and light on empirical research. Many of the studies in the text generalized broadly from anecdotal, biographical, and/or small samples of multiracial people. We draw attention to this text precisely because it *was* the cutting-edge research on biracial people at the time it was published. In essence, the census debate occurred on an empirically shaky foundation, creating a space in which impassioned personal testimony took on the weight of scientific data.

The primary reason why we undertook this project was to address the scarcity of empirical research that informed the 2000 census debate. We believed at the time, and continue to believe, that critical decisions about racial categorization simply cannot be based on the emotional testimony of individuals. Nor can these decisions be based on the findings of a number of disconnected, small interview studies. Instead, we desired to create a large database of biracial respondents to investigate how, in fact, biracial people understand their racial identity and what social factors influence their choices. The goal of this book, then, is to provide analysis of a quantity of data that has heretofore been unavailable and to provide the quality of analysis that enables answers to important and enduring questions about racial identity. The addition of a multiracial category will unquestionably emerge once again as preparations are made for the 2010 census; therefore, our hope for this project is twofold. First, we hope that this study will open a new path toward a more empirically based and less emotionally laden discourse on multiracialism. Second, and more important, we hope that the findings reported in this book will open up the debate about a multiracial category in the 2010 census to a more dynamic, multifaceted understanding of what biracial identity means to members of this population.

Although it is not one of the primary goals of this text, we also hope that our work is of interest to parents of biracial children. Specifically, we anticipate that our documentation of the broad spectrum of ways that biracial people identify will help parents better understand the effects of decisions they make about where they live and with whom they interact, as well as the power of their discussions with their children about race and identity in America.

Identity in Black and White

One of the difficulties facing the debate over a multiracial category is the question of labels and terminology. To conduct empirical research on biracial identity, we had to first answer the following questions: (a) Who is biracial? (b) What does this term mean? (c) Is biracialism a one-generation or multigenerational phenomenon? and (d) What racial combinations should be considered? We chose to answer these questions by focusing on individuals who have one self-identifying black biological parent and one self-identifying white biological parent. In other words, we excluded anyone who is adopted, anyone whose parents racially self-identify as multiracial, and/or anyone who may be biracial but whose parents are not black and white. On one hand, this narrow definition of biracial bars us from exploring the dynamics of other racial combinations and the ways in which there may be similarities among multiracial people with various racial backgrounds. It also may perpetuate the stereotype that biracial is equivalent to black/white, as opposed to the myriad other potential combinations. We believe that limitation is offset by the analytic clarity that we gain by focusing on only one parental race combination.

Of all the possible multiracial groups we could have chosen, we focused on the offspring of black/white interracial unions. We did so because, in the United States, blacks and whites continue to be the two groups with the greatest social distance, the most spatial separation, and the strongest taboos against interracial marriage. Although the number of interracial marriages has increased dramatically over the past several decades and those unions have become more socially acceptable, black/white marriages still compose a relatively small number of interracial marriages in the United States. That relative rarity is a testament to the continued social stigmatization of intermarriage between blacks and whites. In addition, focusing on black/white biracials enables us to engage profound and enduring questions about racial categorization. Specifically, probing into racial identity among black/white biracials leads to questions about the meaning of race, the efficacy of racial categorization, and how and why Americans have persistently used the "one-drop rule" to determine who is black in America. For no other racial group has the question of racial group membership been so rigidly defined, legally codified, and historically long-standing as it has been for African Americans. Nor has any other racial group been as vocal and adamant in its opposition to the potential addition of a multiracial category.

We also acknowledge the fact that terminology simply does not exist to describe the multiracial population. We have taken commonly used (and confused) terms and attempted to define them in highly specific ways. For our purposes, the term *biracial* refers to any individual with one black and one white parent, irrespective of that person's racial self-identification. We use the term to denote parentage, as opposed to self-understanding, to allow for the possibility that people who have one black and one white parent may racially identify themselves in a variety of different ways. We recognize that this term is commonly used to denote individuals of various combinations; however, for the sake of simplicity, we use the term biracial, as opposed to *black/white biracial*. Throughout the text, the term multiracial is be used to indicate any individual with parents of two different races. This term is intended to be broader in scope than biracial, including mixed-race people of all combinations. In addition, we use the terms *mulatto, quadroon,* and *octoroon* when they are historically appropriate and *mixed* and *high yelluh* in the context of quoting respondents' use of those terms.

This project began in 1996 as a thought piece presented at the North Central Sociological Association's annual meeting. The authors were overwhelmed, and continue to be overwhelmed, by the amount of interest it has generated among academics, politicians, therapists, journalists, parents, and multiracial people. It has required the generous assistance of many to bring this project to its present state. In that way, it represents a collaborative effort not just between the two authors but between the two of us and the many people who have provided us with intellectual, administrative, moral, and emotional support throughout the lengthy process of data collection and analysis and the writing of this book. Of course, any mistakes, flaws, or shortcomings in this work are entirely our own.

Richard Lamanna, Lyn Spillman, Richard Williams, and Andrew Weigert read numerous drafts of this manuscript and responded tirelessly to our calls for advice. We are especially indebted to our colleagues in our writing groups at the University of Notre Dame, Elizabeth Schaefer-Caniglia and Michael Davern; and at Pepperdine University, Jeanne Heffernan, Lyn Reynolds, Reagan Schaffer, and Robert Schaeffer. We thank also those who have read and commented on various drafts and chapters of this book: Khahn Bui, Rainier Spencer, Roland Smith, Flo Mattita, Mitch Berbrier, Bhavani Sitaraman, and the anonymous reviewers who provided invaluable feedback on the original draft of the manuscript.

Steve Monsma and Dan Caldwell provided enormous help in the writing of the initial proposal for this book. David Baird, Dean of Seaver College at Pepperdine University, provided us with resources and encouragement when we most needed it. We especially thank our many colleagues who engaged us in enlightening conversations throughout the years, challenging our assumptions and transforming our thinking: Thorrodur Bjarnason, Amy Orr, Michelle Janning, Arul Arokiasamy, Tarek Joseph, Estelle McNair, Danielle Pollage, Jonathan Coredero, and Tracey Lazloffy.

This project has benefited greatly from the guiding hand of our editor, Jim Brace-Thompson. His enthusiastic response to our research and belief in the necessity of this book also helped bring this project to completion.

We are deeply indebted to the thoughts and ideas that have preceded us and to the researchers who have dedicated their careers to asking questions about racial identity. We hope that this book will keep the conversation going.

Recognition and thanks are also due to William Haupricht and Rachel Orton. Both have helped immeasurably to create a healthy and positive atmosphere that has made the writing of this book, and much of what we do, possible. We are grateful to them both for not only keeping our lives and households running but helping us maintain our sense of humor.

Finally, we offer great thanks to our respondents. This book could not have been written without all those who gave their time and effort to this project by expressing, some for the first time, what it is like to be biracial in America. Without their generosity and willingness to share their intimate personal experiences, this work would fail to exist. Thank you.

1

Who Is Black?

*Flux and Change in
American Racial Identity*

Early in the 1990s, a coalition of mixed-race individuals and advocacy groups from across the nation lobbied the Office of Management and Budget (OMB) for the addition of a multiracial category to the 2000 census. The request was not denied outright. Instead, a lengthy period of public debate ensued over the proposed adjustment to existing racial classifications. After a three-year study, a multiagency governmental task force recommended that the OMB reject the proposed multiracial category. While the need for reliable data on racial groups is ongoing; the addition of more categories was deemed both unnecessary and divisive. As a compromise, the 2000 census enabled individuals to check more than one racial category if they desired. The compromise plan, which was adopted for the collection of all government data on race, received unanimous support from thirty federal agencies including the U.S. Bureau of the Census, the Department of Justice, and the National Center for Health Statistics.[1]

Support for the multiracial initiative was led by grassroots organizations such as Project RACE and the Association of MultiEthnic Americans. These advocacy groups argued for the creation of a new racial category for both demographic and cultural reasons. Their demographic justification cited the trend toward increasing interracial marriages and births of mixed-race children in the United States. In the past three decades, the number of interracial marriages in the United States has increased from 300,000 to 1.4 million, and these households (in addition to cohabiting interracial households) have spawned a boom in the mixed-race population.[2] Their other argument was that mixed-race individuals view themselves as multiracial rather than as belonging exclusively to the racial group of one of their parents. The addition of a multiracial category, its advocates argued, was essential to accurately represent existing demographic shifts in the population *and* to provide a true reflection of biracial people's understanding of their racial identity. For some multiracial advocates, increasing numbers of mixed-race people represent the need for a new social consciousness that permits greater fluidity in the way individuals racially identify themselves.[3]

Leading the opposition to the mixed-race initiative were well-known civil rights leaders, such as Jesse Jackson, Kweisi Mfume (representing the Congressional Black Caucus), and representatives of the NAACP. They argued that the underlying purpose of legislative directives mandating the collection of data on racial groups was to enable the enforcement of civil rights legislation and to document the existence of racial inequalities. Adding a multiracial category, they argued, would increase the difficulty of collecting accurate data on the effects of discrimination and, therefore, deviated from the legal directive given to the Census Bureau.[4]

The current demand for a multiracial category illustrates the arbitrariness of racial classification itself. The history of racial classification also provides evidence that racial classification is a social and cultural process, not a biological, genetic one.[5] Debates surrounding census racial classification, as well as changes in the census questions on race, are not new. In fact, there were eight racial categories in the 1890 census, five in the 1900 census, and eight again in both the 1910 and 1920 censuses. In 1930, the census included ten racial designations, including white, Negro, Indian, Chinese, Japanese, and four new ones that the two previous censuses did not have: Mexican, Filipino, Hindu, and Korean. Mexican, as a racial designation, was not included in 1940, whereas the 1950 census racial classification schema omitted Hindus and Koreans and changed the term *Indian* to read *American Indian*. Eleven categories were possible in 1960 with Hawaiians, Part Hawaiians, Aleuts, and Eskimos added (these last three were deleted by 1970, that year's census having nine racial designations). Furthermore, in 1960, all people of Latin ancestry were to be considered white by interviewers unless they were "clearly" Negro, Indian, or some other "race." The two most recent censuses, 1980 and 1990, provided 15 options for racial designation.[6] At each juncture, debates surrounding the existing racial categorizations in federal censuses have flourished, rooted in social, cultural, and political controversy.[7] The current debate is no exception. It is precisely the enigmatic nature of racial classifications over time that illustrates their social as opposed to biological reality.

The debate surrounding the possible addition of a multiracial category to the 2000 census was an important development because at its foundation, the debate questioned deeply held American assumptions about miscegenation and racial identity. Although there are many more multiracial people in the United States today than at any previous time in our country's history, the demographic argument raised by multiracial advocates was less penetrating theoretically than the questions raised by their cultural and social-psychological contentions. To be certain, biracialness is not a newly emergent social phenomenon. What is new, however, is the way in which advocates claimed that people understand being multiracial in America. Most intriguing about the mobilization of advocacy groups, and the deeply entrenched opposition they encountered in trying to change the census racial categorizations, is that it highlights the latest twist in the ongoing sociohistorical problem of classifying mixed-race people in the United States and, more pointedly, in answering the question: Who is black? We will add to this ongoing discourse by reporting research in this book that focuses exclusively on black/white biracials, those individuals who are the offspring of one black parent and one white parent.

Racial groups in the United States have historically been stratified, and this stratification has been supported by an ideological belief in genetic differentiation among races. Given this stratification, American society has developed a norm to classify individuals who straddle the socially constructed boundaries of black and white. In other words, Americans created a systematized and legally codified answer to the question, Who is black? This classification norm is formally referred to as *hypodescent* by anthropologists, but it is more commonly known as the "one-drop rule." This rule mandates that a mixed-race child shall be relegated to the racial group of the lower-status parent. In practice, this norm has been applied most directly to the African American population as compared to other racial minority groups. The implication is that one drop of black ancestry contaminates an individual, precluding that person from ever being "purely" white.

The one-drop rule is firmly grounded in historical tradition, but more important, it has served as a cultural base supporting racial inequalities. Because this social and cultural norm is at the very foundation of the question, Who is black? and because our understanding of biracial identity rests on the answer to this question, it is important to explore the emergence, ideological purpose, and historical trajectory of the one-drop rule.

The Beginnings of Miscegenation

Miscegenation has occurred in the United States as long as individuals from African and European populations have had contact. Race mixing, as well as the one-drop rule, can be traced back to the colonial period. In the early colonies, particularly in the Chesapeake area, miscegenation occurred largely between white indentured servants and both enslaved and free blacks.[8] These individuals were from the lowest socioeconomic status, and therefore, the practice was seen as a vice of the white underclass.[9] In most colonies, the mixed-race children that resulted from these unions were considered black. A notable exception was Virginia, where mixed-race children were sometimes considered white because a law was enacted stating that any person who had one fourth black ancestry was black. Therefore, some mixed-race people were considered white in Virginia.[10] Because white society viewed miscegenation as unacceptable, the one-drop rule emerged and functioned as an uncodified societal norm.

During this early colonial period, areas in the lower South, especially Louisiana and South Carolina, perceived race mixing differently than their Northern counterparts. Interracial intercourse occurred less frequently in the lower South, and these illicit unions were generally between white men and both enslaved and free black women.[11] Miscegenation was more accepted in these areas, particularly in Charleston, South Carolina, and New Orleans, where free mulattos formed an alliance with whites and served an important role as a buffer group between whites and blacks.[12] It is important to note that in these two geographic locales, mulattos possessed a unique in-between status within the existing racial hierarchy. Because of their buffer status, they developed a strong group identity that was distinct from either whites or blacks.[13]

Slavery and the One-Drop Rule

The institution of slavery was built on a strong white supremacist ideology of racial separation and an absolute social prohibition of miscegenation. The fear underlying anti-miscegenation attitudes was that black blood would taint the purity of the white race. Although whites publicly denounced miscegenation, white men practiced it with regularity.[14] The plantation era brought whites and blacks into close physical proximity on a daily basis. The slave-owning mentality included a belief that white male slave owners had the right to sexually "use" their black female slaves at will. As a result, the vast majority of interracial sex consisted of exploitative unions between white male slave owners and their black female slaves.[15] Sexual intercourse between white women and black male slaves was strictly forbidden, in part, because of the possibility of that union producing a mixed-race child. To have a mulatto child in a white family was scandalous and threatened the entire ideological logic of the slave system. A mixed-race child in the slave quarters, however, was not only tolerated but was considered an economic asset.[16] As miscegenation between whites and blacks continued, in addition to the sexual unions between mulatto and unmixed black slaves, the black population gradually "whitened." By the end of slavery, there existed a diversity of physical traits among blacks, ranging from unmixed African blacks to whites.[17]

There were clear and obvious incentives for plantation owners to classify their mixed-race children as black. Although they were relegated to slave status, many times light-skinned mulatto children of the master were given special privileges.[18] These privileges included work in the master's house (as opposed to the more demanding work in the fields), an education, training in the skilled trades, and access to the white culture. Overall, the one-drop rule was the unquestioned norm in the plantation-dominated South.

The exceptions to the one-drop rule, which both challenged and contradicted it as the existing racial classification norm, occurred in

Charleston and New Orleans. As previously mentioned, free mulattos in these two regions had aligned themselves with whites and willingly served as a buffer between whites and free and enslaved blacks. As the Civil War approached, white southerners became increasingly defensive of slavery and rallied in support of the one-drop rule. This defensive posture created a climate of distrust and hostility toward free mulattos throughout the southern states and permanently altered the relationship between whites and mulattos in these two deviant locales. The severed ties between these two groups sent free mulattos seeking alliances with blacks and shifted their sense of identity accordingly.[19]

The Civil War caused existing ideological divisions to become even more deeply entrenched. The socially constructed boundaries between blacks and whites were reinforced as national attention was focused on the war, which had the institution of slavery squarely at its center. At the war's conclusion, southern whites accepted the one-drop rule without question, because they tended to view all blacks as the enemy.[20] Mulattos became even more closely aligned with blacks during the war due to their increased alienation from whites and to the fact that many whites viewed them as part of the black race.[21] Many mulattos were free prior to the conclusion of the Civil War and, therefore, tended to be better educated and more skilled than the newly freed blacks; many emerged as leaders of southern blacks and served in the critically important roles of teachers, relief administrators, missionaries, and legislators.[22] This complete alliance between mulattos and southern blacks resulted in full acceptance of the one-drop rule by all members of the American population. Whites, blacks, and mulattos, for varying reasons, all came to full agreement that the one-drop rule was the answer to the question, Who is black?

Jim Crow and the Protection of White Womanhood

The Jim Crow system of segregation was built on the landmark legal case, *Plessy v. Ferguson*, in 1896. This case established the doctrine of "separate but equal" throughout the country and enabled a clear and unequivocal distinction to be made between the social worlds of blacks and whites. The passing of a multitude of segregation and anti-miscegenation laws in most states necessitated a legal definition of who, precisely, belonged in the category black. At this moment in history, the one-drop rule, previously an informal norm, was legally codified.[23] The result of this legal codification was to make *de jure* a previously *de facto* cultural and social norm that had, for generations, dictated interactions between the races since the first slaves arrived in America.

While society was preoccupied with racial boundary maintenance, mulattos continued to be considered members of the black community.[24] The political struggle against segregation was led by prominent mulattos such as W.E.B. Du Bois, William Monroe Trotter, James Weldon Johnson, A. Philip Randolph, and Walter White. The complete identification of mulattos with the black community was further illustrated in the Harlem Renaissance (1923-1930). In this artistic celebration of the black American experience, the total and complete internalization of the one-drop rule by both blacks and mulattos was evident.[25] This is clear because the work of mulatto artists, musicians, dancers, poets, and writers was *the* articulation of the black experience.[26] Included among these prominent and gifted artists were Zora Neal Hurston, Langston Hughes, Claude McKay, and Jean Toomer, names and people whom historians simply remember as black.

During the period of segregation, interracial sexual contacts decreased significantly and were restricted, almost exclusively, to white male exploitation of black women. Segregation raised the specter of "white womanhood" as the ultimate justification of anti-miscegenation laws. These images were represented in the mainstream media, most saliently captured in the popular movie *Birth of a Nation*. In one scene, a white virgin is being chased by a black man to the edge of a cliff, where she must decide the lesser of two evils, being (presumably) raped by her black pursuer or throwing herself off the cliff. She jumps to her death, sending a powerful message about miscegenation.

The taboo against intercourse between black men and white women was strong and backed by an informal system of violent sanctions, the most common of which was lynching. Not unlike their behavior during the days of slavery, white men publicly decried miscegenation in defense of white womanhood but privately engaged in interracial sex. This contradictory stance was supported by the one-drop rule, because a mulatto child could be accepted in a black family without question.

The One-Drop Rule
and Civil Rights

The system of segregation was doomed by the precedent-setting decision of *Brown v. Board of Education* in 1954. This decision nullified the spirit of the separate-but-equal doctrine previously established in *Plessy v. Fergeson*, which had been reinforced by numerous, increasingly restrictive state segregation laws thereafter. Desegregation in the Deep South was initiated slowly until the Supreme Court decided in 1969 *(Alexander v. Holmes County Board of Education)* that no further delays in the desegregation of schools would be tolerated and that southern schools must draft realistic plans for desegregation immediately.[27] Passage of the Civil Rights Act of 1964, the Voting Rights Act in 1965, and legislative protections against housing discrimination in 1968 legally tore down barriers for blacks but did not provide instant social integration. Although these legal barriers were dismantled, de facto segregation remained alive and well in both the North and South.[28]

In addition to continued de facto segregation, blacks faced considerable white backlash in reaction to court-enforced desegregation. The result of the backlash was increased unity within the black population and the emergence of "black pride" and "black power" in the late 1960s. This intense period of group unity produced a strong sense of black identity and pride in African American culture. In this emotional climate of racial polarization, mulattos, who had led the earlier renaissance, were stigmatized.[29] Whereas light skin and a white appearance had been assets toward upward mobility within the black community in earlier periods, they lost their value and became a cultural liability.[30] This is best captured in Geneva Smitherman's description of the term "high yelluh":

A very light-complexioned African American; praised in some quarters, damned in others. Community ambivalence stems from *high yelluhs'* close physical approximation to European Americans. To the extent that white skin is valued, as was the case, for example, in the 1940s and 1950s, then being *yelluh* is a plus. On the other hand, to the extent that a *yelluh* African is a reminder of whiteness/the "enemy," as was the case in the Black Power Movement of the 1960s and 1970s, for instance, then being *yelluh* is a minus.[31]

Mulattos walked a fine line in these tumultuous times. The more the country focused on the "race problem," the more deeply Americans viewed race as an absolute biological as opposed to a socially constructed reality and the more unquestioned the one-drop rule became. Miscegenation continued throughout these times, although marriage increasingly became an option after the Supreme Court ruled in 1967 *(Loving V. Commonwealth of Virginia)* that state laws prohibiting interracial marriages were unconstitutional.[32] In the early 1960s, twenty-two states still had anti-miscegenation laws. By the mid-1960s and 1970s, interracial marriages had increased in number; however, marriages between blacks and whites accounted for less than 1 percent of all marriages. Mixed-race people remained fully aligned with blacks, despite the fact that some (especially those who appeared white) experienced negative treatment by blacks in the climate of black power.

Mixed-Race People in the Post-Civil Rights Era

Despite legal advances made for the entire African American community, mixed-raced individuals were more socially mobile than those of darker skin.[33] Whereas racial solidarity was increasingly important for most African Americans, mixed-raced individuals continued to move up in the U.S. social hierarchy. The privileges bestowed on this group due to their light complexions enabled upward economic mobility.

The privileges secured by mulattos from whites during the slavery era set the tone for a generational advantage for those who were mixed.[34] The advantage, termed the *intergenerational drag* by Robert Margo or the *social origins explanation* by Mark Hill, refers to the greater social mobility of lighter-skinned blacks and mulattos, which came from the higher propensity of mulattos to be better educated, to be trained in skilled occupations, and to have more access to the dominant white culture than other slaves who were not mixed race.[35] Indeed, free mulattos tended to replicate white culture as closely as possible, which resulted in a sense of elitism that endured over many generations.[36] Because of this advantage over other blacks, many mulattos held positions of importance and more socially acceptable roles and occupations. The fact that mulattos and lighter-skinned blacks have garnered social and material advantages over their darker-skinned counterparts has been documented by both early and contemporary social researchers.[37]

Cultural Norms and Support of Racial Stratification

When classifying human beings in discrete categories is critical to the maintenance of social relations within a society, norms emerge to establish strict boundary maintenance.[38] Throughout the history of race relations in the United States, racial group membership has been a critical identity marker affecting the life chances and mobility of individuals. At the heart of the varying systems of racial stratification lies the critical question, Who is black in America? A patterned answer emerges from the previous historical analysis. That answer can be found by examining the existing stratification system of each time period. The one-drop rule emerged to support the system of slavery in the southern states. It became more deeply entrenched in the minds of southern whites as slavery became threatened and was forcibly dissolved. This classification norm served equally well to justify the inequalities of legalized segregation while simultaneously allowing for continued miscegenation between white men and black women. As legalized segregation was dismantled, racial discrimination continued, with the one-drop rule as the unquestioned assumption of racial categorization.

It is also necessary to consider the interplay between societal pressures for racial boundary maintenance and group responses to the parameters of identity set forth. Within this complex dynamic, we can begin to see clearly how identity functions as a social process. American history provides unusual cases where regional cultures deviated from the one-drop rule. Such cases enable us to see the social psychological processes of identity development at work in varying normative circumstances. New Orleans and Charleston were previously mentioned as deviating from the one-drop rule; in these places, historians argue that mulattos were closely aligned with whites prior to the Civil War, forming a buffer group between blacks and whites. In these two cases, mulattos developed a racial identity that corresponded to their social location as a separate group. This option was possible because the dominant group both provided and accepted an alternative racial identity for mulattos. An in-between status was impossible elsewhere because whites would not allow mulattos to exist as a buffer group. With the alternative option in place in Charleston and New Orleans, mulattos developed an understanding of themselves *as mulattos* and viewed their relationship to others as a separate racial group.

The self-identity of mulattos (as mulattos) in both Charleston and New Orleans changed drastically as American society engaged in the Civil War. Their long-standing alliance with whites disintegrated as their buffer status and separate identity became socially unacceptable in the racially polarized South. Mulattos in these two cities became more closely aligned with blacks as society, increasingly accepting the one-drop rule as absolute, viewed them as part of the black race. Because the separate mulatto identity was no longer available, their self-understanding shifted within the changing parameters. By the time of the Harlem Renaissance of the 1920s, mulattos were universally considered a part of the black community. They had so fully accepted a black racial identity that they were at the cutting edge in artistic expression of the meaning of the black experience in America.

A historical view allows us to see several key features that are fundamental to an understanding of racial identity. First and foremost, racial identities are socially constructed and maintained to support existing social relations. The preservation of these categories is difficult due to the fact that they are grounded in a social as opposed to a biological reality. An elaborate series of assumptions, rules, and laws is required to maintain these categories. Inevitably, individuals exist who defy the dichotomous classification, and their identity will depend on the existing status of race relations. American society has followed this pattern in the past. However, as African Americans make economic gains, middle-class integration becomes more widespread, and interracial marriages increase, how do the changing intergroup relations affect the way biracial people are viewed by society? In other words, how does the changing nature of racial stratification in today's society affect the way in which those individuals who defy dichotomous classification are socially categorized and come to understand their own racial identity?

Assimilation Versus Egalitarian Pluralism

The term *assimilation* is usually reserved for discussions of white ethnic groups, referring to the social processes by which groups enter a new society and gradually become part of that society by shedding the culture of their native land. Assimilation is considered to be a gradual process, one that occurs more successfully the more time an individual or group has spent in the new country. It was once believed that for European immigrants, ethnic identity would cease to remain a salient category of self-understanding because individuals would so thoroughly become part of their new culture, particularly after several generations, that they would no longer need to identify with their country of origin.[39]

Successful assimilation of immigrant groups depends on the reduction of structural barriers.[40] It has been argued that if members of an ethnic group are residentially segregated, discriminated against in the labor market, and restricted in their social networks, their ethnic identity will remain strong. If, however, those structural barriers are decreased or disappear altogether, ethnic group membership will no longer be salient.[41] Instead, other types of identity will become more important to individuals as categories of self-understanding. One key indicator of how successfully a group has assimilated is the group's rate of intermarriage. Decreasing importance of ethnic identity increases willingness and likelihood of marriage outside the ethnic group. Therefore, high intermarriage rates indicate successful ethnic group assimilation.

The term assimilation is used sparingly with racial groups and almost never in reference to African Americans. In part, this is due to the white racism underlying the one-drop rule. The result was that "passing" was the only option for blacks to shed their racial group membership. The term *passing* refers to the practice of crossing the socially constructed color line to live as a white person, an option only available to African Americans with physical features that would allow them to be identified as white. Passing came into existence during slavery and increased in frequency during the Jim Crow period.[42] Individual African Americans chose to pass to escape discrimination and increase employment opportunities. The costs of passing, however, were high, including emotional stress from cutting ties to family, condemnation from some segments of the black community, and the constant fear of being "discovered" by whites. Many who passed did so only for a short period of time and returned to the black community. As structural barriers fell in later decades, opportunities for upward mobility increased, and occurrences of passing decreased (although they did not disappear altogether). Because of the one-drop rule, crossing the color line in the form of passing was the only way for African

Americans to leave their racial group, and it was a tenuous and complicated option at best. Furthermore, it was an option primarily reserved for those of mixed-race ancestry whose physical appearance allowed classification as white.

Intermarriage, as the mechanism enabling assimilation for white ethnic and non-black racial groups, has been unavailable to African Americans, legally and later culturally. Given this blocked path, assimilation has never been a goal in the same way it was for white ethnic groups. More specifically, because of the white supremacist belief in the biological purity of the white race, African Americans were not placed on the assimilation path. Since the 1970s, black leaders have conceptualized an egalitarian pluralism, not assimilation, as the goal for black-white race relations. This egalitarian pluralism includes equal treatment, freedom from discrimination, mutual respect of all racial and ethnic groups, and retention of group identity.[43] It is a very different proposition from the vision of assimilation previously described. Building on Milton Gordon's distinction between structural assimilation and cultural assimilation, it could be argued that egalitarian pluralism is a push by black leaders toward structural assimilation without giving way to cultural assimilation.[44] Our use of the term assimilation in the context of this book encompasses both cultural and structural factors, so that groups we refer to as *assimilated* are those that no longer experience structural barriers associated with their ethnic group status, nor are they culturally distinct from whites.

The move to add a multiracial category to the U.S. census provides some evidence of both mixed-race individuals and white women (on behalf of their children) demanding a separate racial status. Advocates can be generally characterized as middle-class, living in racially heterogeneous neighborhoods, and wanting to be considered distinct from both whites and blacks.[45] Their multiracial agenda implies a different answer to the question, Who is black? and their answer both is an explicit rejection of the one-drop rule and has been portrayed as a movement toward both cultural and racial assimilation. This agenda, particularly its implied assimilationist goal, has been most passionately objected to by leaders of the black community. Underlying their legalistically framed opposition is a threat of a decreased census count, which has real political and financial consequences. At a deeper level, however, there exists an open hostility toward the idea that mixed-race people may want to distinguish themselves as separate from the black community. It seems worthwhile to quote at length Molefi Kete Asante, an ardent Afrocentrist, as he distinctly articulates his opposition, not to the addition of a multiracial category to the census but to the *idea* of mixed-race identity:

> One cannot read magazines like *New People* and *Interrace* without getting the idea that self-hatred among some African Americans is at an all-time high. Both of these magazines, founded by interracial couples and appealing most to interracial families, see themselves as the vanguard to explode racial identity by claiming to be a third race in addition to African and European. Of course, in the context of a racist society the white parent wishes for his/her offspring the same privileges that he/she has enjoyed often at the expense of Africans. However, the offspring is considered by tradition, custom, appearance, and history to be black. In a white racist society blackness is considered a negative attribute which carries with it the burden of history and discrimination. Thus, the *New People* and the *Interrace* group attempt to minimize the effects of blackness by claiming that they are neither white nor black, but colored. The nonsense in this position is seen when we consider the fact that nearly 70 percent of all African Americans are genetically mixed with either Native Americans or whites. The post-Du Bois, and perhaps more accurately, the post-Martin Luther King, Jr., phenomenon of seeking to explode racial identity has two prongs: one is white guilt and the other is black self-hatred. In the case of interracial families one often sees the urgent need to provide the offspring with a race other than that defined by custom, tradition, appearance, and history.[46]

This statement articulates the underlying frustration of some opponents of the multiracial category. Asante's comments force a questioning of where race relations stand in post–civil rights America. He suggests that a negative consequence of the discourse on race is the emergence of the myth that, at the turn of the millennium, race no longer matters. However, the mere desire of white parents for their children to be identified as mixed-race (as opposed to black) signifies an implied acknowledgment that racial groups exist, that they exist in a hierarchy, and that separation from the subordinate group brings an individual closer to the dominant group. Opponents view the demand of advocates for a new racial category, in combination with their middle-class economic status, as a movement with an assimilationist ideological underpinning.

What is critical to this tension between multiracial advocates and leaders of the black community is the racial self-understanding of biracial people. In other words, it is less important whether or not biracial people appear black "on the outside," it's how they understand themselves "on the inside" that counts. Black identity is not characterized by physical traits because members of the black community have an enormous variety of physical appearance, including those who physically appear white. Instead, black identity is conceptualized as developing out of the common experience of being black in America. Black leaders point to the numerous people who may have one black and one white parent, yet experience the world as black people and are understood by others in society as members of the black community.[47] As Asante stated, biracial children are "considered by tradition, custom, appearance, and history to be black."

In contrast, leaders of the multiracial movement point to the push for self-determination by individuals who understand their racial identity not as black in accordance with the one-drop rule, but as "biracial." They argue that being biracial is a unique experience that is different from being black. According to activists, individuals, regardless of physical appearance, experience the world from the unique perspective of being mixed-race; have common experiences with blacks, whites, and other biracial people; and are understood by others as biracial (not exclusively as black). To have a biracial self-understanding, this identity must be validated by others in their social environment. It is precisely this claim of validation that leads individuals to believe that the category has meaning and is a necessary addition to the existing racial landscape.

Understanding the tension between interest groups and, at the broadest level, the competing visions of the future of black-white race relations is critical to grasping the profound importance of a potentially new answer to the very old question, Who is black? For both parties in the census debate, understanding biracial identity is critical. Each perspective holds a differing and singular view of how mixed-race people understand their place in America's racial system. Their positions are fundamentally dependent on how people within the emerging mixed-race population understand their racial identity.

This book is an examination of the dynamic meaning of racial identity for black/white biracial people in the United States and asks the question, What does biracial identity mean to individuals within this population?

We explore the varying choices biracial people make about their racial identity and propose an explanatory model of the social factors predicting why these individuals make drastically different choices about who they are. Our explanatory model includes socialization, contextual and interactional factors that we explore using both in-depth interview and survey data.

There have been few attempts to synthesize and/or review the rapidly proliferating body of empirical research on biracial identity. This research spans the disciplinary boundaries of developmental and clinical psychology, sociology, demography, cultural studies, and philosophy. We work to remedy this in Chapter 2, where we review the empirical literature on the biracial experience to provide the reader with a foundation for our research design. We then describe our data collection strategy in detail, focusing on how we attempted to overcome several of the most prominent methodological limitations in the existing literature while addressing the most enduring questions about biracial identity.

Chapter 3 provides a descriptive account of the multiple ways in which mixed-race people understand what biracial identity means, drawing heavily on interview data to create a conceptual map of existing possibilities for racial self-understanding. In this chapter, we present the typology of racial understandings for biracial people that emerged from our data analysis. In so doing, we challenge existing assumptions of multiracial advocates, researchers, and civil rights leaders that there exists a unified definition of biracial identity.

One key element of these varying experiences of biracial people's lives is their socialization experiences. Because socialization variables play a critical role in the development and maintenance of racial identities, Chapter 4 focuses on social and structural factors that distinguish among the types of identities presented in Chapter 3. This chapter provides a thorough analysis of how early childhood experiences, family socialization, and social network composition predict the variation in racial identity choice among biracial people.

Chapter 5 pushes for further theoretical depth by illustrating the crucial function of appearance in the selection of racial identity options. It is assumed that physical appearance determines racial identity, serving as one of the key cues demarcating racial group membership. Contrary to this commonsense notion, the results in this chapter demonstrate the power of social interaction in the way that individuals perceive their embodied self.

We show in this chapter that although appearance is an influential predictor of what type of racial identity biracial respondents develop, it is mediated, at times dramatically so, by the way that individuals experience race in their daily lives and interactions with others.

The final chapter (Chapter 6) reflects on the economic and political context that has created an environment for the emergence of multiple new understandings of biracial identity and the potential ramifications that newly emergent categories may have for race relations in the United States. Specifically, we return to the question, Who is black? by examining how the politics underlying the 2000 census debate were informed by differential ideas about the reality of race in America. We also ponder the future of the one-drop rule in light of the lived experiences of our biracial respondents.

Ultimately, this book seeks to answer what it means to be biracial in contemporary American society and how that meaning is fundamentally shaped by the culture in which people live. We do this by listening to the voices of biracial people. This perspective, often neglected in debates over governmental categorization, is essential to developing a comprehensive understanding of how individual identity development occurs within the context of cultural and structural constraints.

2

Biracial Identity Research

Past and Present

Research on the biracial population is a diverse and multidisciplinary body of work. Empirical efforts to understand what biracial identity means and how individuals come to develop their individual racial self-understanding(s) include a vast array of theoretical and methodological approaches. In this chapter, we provide an overview of existing studies, with an eye toward drawing out the major questions, theoretical frameworks, and significant findings of this broad and somewhat unwieldy collection of disparate parts.

It is inherently useful to understand how research on biracial identity has developed and changed over time; however, we propose this overview primarily as a foundation for an explanatory discussion of our research design. We highlight the important findings and the methodological strengths and weaknesses inherent in the existing body of work as a way of providing a context for our research design, which was an attempt to improve on the serious methodological flaws in the existing literature while addressing some of the most enduring questions. Our intention for this study was to build on the extant research by unifying some of its theoretically divergent parts while simultaneously taking a methodological leap forward.

We begin with an overview of studies on biracial identity with exclusive attention given to those that focus on black/white biracials. While we recognize that researchers have focused on a variety of different groups and racial combinations under the overarching conceptual term *multiracial,* this variation has produced a lack of clarity. When combined with the use of widely discrepant measures, drawing generalizations and comparisons across studies is extremely difficult. Therefore, we review only studies that have black/white biracial participants. The methodological limitations and empirical patterns are then highlighted as a transition to an explanation of our research design.

To review the literature, we conducted an extensive search to locate journal articles, books, and book chapters from the various branches of psychology, sociology, anthropology, and social work that empirically investigated black/white biracial identity in adolescents or adults in the United States. There are a number of things we did not include. We did not include work that was entirely theoretical or conceptual, although it is important to note that this characterizes the majority of academic writing on biracial identity. We also excluded dissertations, conference papers, or other unpublished work. A total of thirty-one studies met our review criteria.

The primary characteristic of empirical research on biracial identity is *diversity.* Authors of the studies we reviewed used a vast array of theoretical frameworks (or none at all), methodological approaches, and conceptual definitions of biracial. Given the degree of methodological and conceptual variation, it is no surprise that the findings are often inconclusive or contradictory. This overview is a descriptive effort to pull together what is known about biracial identity above and beyond personal biography, conceptual essays, and social advocacy.

Definitions of Biracial Identity

Most of the empirical studies that were examined for this analysis offered no conceptual definition of biracial identity. Some authors narrowed the term *biracial* to describe the specific racial combinations of their respondents (i.e., only black/white biracials), whereas others qualified the term biracial by making the distinction between first- and second-generation children of interracial couples. Another approach was to use the term biracial only after acknowledging that the concept of race was biologically unsubstantiated but accepting its use as a socially constructed organizing principle nonetheless.

Although conceptual definitions of biracial identity were not explicitly stated in most empirical studies, implicit assumptions about biracial identity were often embedded in the overall structure of the research design. These assumptions followed a historical trajectory from absolute and unspoken adherence to the one-drop rule to a refutation of the one-drop rule as a cultural norm.

The history of identity exploration within the African American population is well documented and important to consider when discussing biracial identity because, prior to the 1960s, biracial identity was equivalent to black identity.[1] Researchers operating under the assumptions of the one-drop rule considered all those who had any African ancestry to fall into the category black. Therefore, theoretical frameworks and research designs that were intended for blacks were assumed to apply to biracial people. As a corollary, no psychological distinctions were made between black and biracial respondents in terms of their racial identity.

In the 1960s, a few researchers began to view biracial people as a subsample of blacks. However, these studies focused on understanding how biracial individuals developed a black identity. By the mid 1980s and throughout the 1990s, the alleged pathologies associated with biracial individuals' marginality drew the attention of a new generation of researchers, who sought to explain psychologically, clinically, and developmentally how these individuals developed a biracial identity and how they could maintain a healthy, integrated sense of their biracialism.[2] The 1990s brought yet another generation of scholars exclusively interested in the lives of biracial people. These investigators used new analytical tools and incorporated interdisciplinary approaches. Their work stood in opposition to earlier studies that assumed biracials to be equivalent to, or a subset of, African Americans. Instead, the new researchers (many of whom were multiracial and/or multiracial activists) assumed that biracial people were a separate group worthy of study with unique, although nonpathological identity issues.

Theoretical Frameworks for the Study of Biracial Identity

There appear to be two dominant theoretical frameworks that have been used in research on the biracial population, although 65 percent of the studies we reviewed had no theoretical framework whatsoever. Some of the atheoretical articles are consciously so, stating that the work is exploratory and taking a grounded theory approach.[3] The remaining work falls into two broad theoretical perspectives: (a) identity formation (psycholanalytic views from developmental and counseling psychology) and (b) symbolic interactionism (used mainly by social psychologists and sociologists). Although the minority of studies fall into these broad frameworks, the extent to which researchers make use of them varies greatly. Below, we briefly describe each of the theoretical perspectives and how they are extended to encompass biracial identity construction and maintenance.

Identity Formation

Many studies of biracial identity use Erik Erikson's developmental framework as a foundation to explain ego-identity formation.[4] According to Erikson, the central task of adolescence is to form a stable identity, or "a sense of personal sameness and historical continuity."[5] This is done by progressing through a variety of exploratory and experimental stages that culminate in a decision, or commitment, in certain areas such as religion, occupation, and political orientation. The formation of racial identity may follow a process similar to the formation of ego identity because individuals explore and make various levels of commitment over time. Numerous conceptual models of black identity have evolved from this perspective, as have untested models specific to biracials.[6]

Both Roger Herring and Jewelle Taylor Gibbs suggest that the challenge for biracial adolescents is twofold.[7] First, they must successfully integrate dual racial and/or cultural identifications while also learning how to develop a positive self-concept and sense of competence. Second, they must develop the ability to synthesize their earlier identifications into a coherent and stable sense of a personal identity as well as a positive racial identity. Both Herring and Gibbs argue that developmental problems may arise when individuals experience conflicts in their efforts to resolve the following five major psychosocial tasks: (a) conflicts about their dual racial/ethnic identity, (b) conflicts about their social marginality, (c) conflicts about their sexuality and choice of sexual partners, (d) conflicts about separation from their parents, and (e) conflicts about their educational or career aspirations. For the most part, researchers using a developmental framework tend to assume that an integrated biracial/bicultural identity is the healthy goal, as opposed to a black identity. Problems are defined as occurring in the process of developing a unified biracial identity. Individuals having a black identity are described as having "overidentified with their black parent" and are considered to have made an unhealthy resolution of developmental issues.[8]

Symbolic Interaction

Sociologists focusing on biracial identity from the microlevel of analysis rely heavily on symbolic interactionism as a paradigmatic frame. Interactionists assume that (a) people know things by their meanings, (b) meanings are created through social interaction, and (c) meanings change through interaction.[9] Given these basic assumptions, *identity* refers to a validated self-understanding that situates and defines an individual or, as Gregory Stone suggests, establishes *what* and *where* an actor is in social terms.[10] Identitiy is a process by which individuals understand themselves and others, as well as evaluate their self in relation to others.

Interactionism draws investigators of biracial identity to focus on microlevel negotiations between actors as the terrain in which identities are either affirmed or negated. Identities, as validated self-understandings, depend on confirmation from others to be developed and maintained by individuals. Therefore, biracial identity as an emergent category of racial identification and classification has the potential to be established, to be stabilized, and to proliferate in the microinteractional sphere, and yet it also may be denied, negated, and further marginalized. Analyses that draw on this tradition tend to rely heavily on social interactions as the contextual networks in which identities emerge and are contested.

Empirical Findings

The studies that we reviewed used various conceptualizations, definitions, operationalizations, and measurement. Systematic comparison among the studies is made problematic by this lack of conceptual and methodological consistency; the findings of these studies are difficult to compare and, at times, contradictory. Given those limitations, it appears that the empirical literature on biracial identity clusters around five basic issues: (a) self-esteem, self-concept, and psychological adjustment; (b) identity in relation to majority culture; (c) appearance; (d) the effect of contextual factors on identity construction; and (e) racial identity development. Each of these issues is discussed in turn.

Self-Esteem, Self-Concept, and Psychological Adjustment

Numerous conceptual studies of biracial identity have considered the relationship of racial group identity and self-concept. In the racial identity literature, debate exists over whether strong group membership leads to positive self-esteem or if identification with a low-status minority group leads to low self-esteem.[11] The relationship between group identity and self-esteem becomes even more complex when, at least theoretically, an individual has the potential for dual group membership. Questions emerge regarding the group with which actors identify. Do they identify with both groups or with neither group? How does each of these potentially different group identifications affect an individual's self-esteem?

In attempts to address core questions of self-concept, some researchers studying biracial respondents have shifted their focus from group identification to *reference group orientation*. Grounded in William Cross's models of black identity (also known as *Nigrescence models*), this subtle distinction creates the conceptual space in which, irrespective of racial group categorization, people may be more oriented toward one group or another.[12] Reference group orientation refers to a person's "participation and enjoyment of the culture of both the black and white communities (e.g., friendships, dating partners, music, and clothing styles)."[13] Hence, there is the possibility of a bicultural orientation.

Lynda Field has examined the relationship between self-concept and reference group orientation for biracial respondents, whereas the research teams of Ana Mari Cauce, Yumi Hiraga, Craig Mason, Tanya Aguilar, Nydia Ordonez, and Nancy Gonzales and of Jewelle Taylor Gibbs and Alice Hines have focused on self-esteem as the primary dependent variable.[14] Interestingly, although these three studies all used psychometrically sound measures of self-worth, they resulted in varied findings about the self-esteem of biracial respondents. In Field's sample of thirty-one biracial respondents, she found that no differences existed between biracial, black, and white respondents in their sense of self-worth. However, biracial teens with a black or bicultural orientation had more positive self-concepts than those who had a white reference group orientation. Cauce and her associates also found no difference between their sample of minority and biracial peers on self-worth, although they did not use a white comparison group. Gibbs and Hines interviewed twelve biracial respondents and found that they had a positive sense of self esteem (again, no comparison group was used).

Other researchers conducting exploratory studies have found a variety of positive psychological traits among samples of biracial respondents. These positive attributes include adaptability, resiliency, and creativity.[15] Such positive psychological outcomes for biracials are associated with competence, high self- esteem, and involvement in supportive social networks.[16]

In contrast to the previously mentioned studies, which paint a positive picture of biracial adjustment, most studies—and, significantly, most early studies—that focus on self-esteem and psychological adjustment issues among biracials have found significant negative outcomes. Separate studies conducted by Milton Gordon, Fernando Henriques, Joyce Ladner, and Vladimir Piskacek and Marlene Golub found that biracial youths have low self-esteem, confused racial or ethnic identity, and psychological or behavioral problems.[17]

The findings comparing biracial people's psychological states to comparable groups of blacks also yield contradictory findings. Whereas both Field and Cauce and her colleagues found no differences among black, white, and biracial respondents on measures of self-esteem, other researchers assert that the self-concepts of biracial people develop differently than those who have a singular racial background.[18] In fact, Piskacek and Golub argue that racial identity formation is more difficult for adolescents from a biracial background than for monoracial adolescents.[19]

Identity in Relation to Majority Culture

Numerous authors have been concerned with the relationship between racial groups in society. Focusing on the biracial population, group relations are greater in complexity because the groups in question are not clearly defined and the intergroup interactions may occur on a daily basis within an interracial household. Of the studies that we reviewed, several addressed the issue of how individuals interact with both majority and minority groups in society.

Within the interracial household, the most prevalent representation of the majority group is the white parent. In most interracial marriages, the white parent is the female partner.[20] Herring found that the potential exists for black/white biracials to identify themselves exclusively as one race or the other, although he considers that to be an "overidentification" with one parent. This finding is supported by Gibbs, whose analysis of a small sample of clinical cases found that overidentification with the black parent may lead to a rejection of white culture and white friends. She argues that individuals may act in an exaggerated manner by "adopting the attitudes, behaviors, styles of dress, and styles of speech stereotypically associated with low-income blacks rather than with their own middle-class life-style." She goes on to observe that

these behaviors not only are quite dissonant with the [middle-class] family life-style but also tend to result in a negative identity formation. That is, the negative identity is associated with the dissonant and devalued social status of the black parent's culture, which is not congruent with the reality of these client's life experiences.[21]

In contrast, the biracial individual may overidentify with the white parent as the symbol of the dominant majority, resulting in a rejection of the black parent. Other researchers have echoed this latter assertion, finding that biracials may have various problems with their minority parent.[22] This dichotomous acceptance/rejection model also seems to be supported by Field's finding that biracials who have a white reference group orientation have more negative feelings about blacks.[23]

Appearance and Identity

Several studies explored the relationship between physical appearance and racial identification among mixed-race respondents. Although this was a main area of explanatory interest in eight of the studies we reviewed, there was no consistent set of findings. Some studies found appearance to be a strongly influential factor in racial identity development, asserting that because most black/white biracials fail to gain acceptance in white society, irrespective of the fairness of their complexion, they most often identify themselves as black.[24] Other studies, however, have found that physical features were overridden by social factors and therefore were irrelevant in the process of identity construction.

Theresa Williams's research focused on biracial people with ambiguous appearance, exploring how they negotiate their identities in everyday social interaction. Among her twenty respondents, she found that individuals reported repeated incidents of being asked "What are you?" by acquaintances and strangers seeking to ascertain their correct racial categorization.[25] Michael Omi and Harold Winant refer to this question, common to the biracial experience, as "a momentary crisis of racial meaning."[26] Williams concluded that individuals "do race" by adjusting to their circumstances, actively negotiating interactional space, and projecting different selves.

Dorcas Bowles reported findings from a group of thirty clinical patients whom she had counseled over a period of thirty years.[27] Among her clinical sample, appearance was important in racial identity construction and held the potentiality for negative psychological outcomes, particularly for women. She contends that the developmental task for biracials is to integrate two ethnic identities and two cultural backgrounds into a single positive ethnic identity. This integration, however, is difficult because an individual's phenotype does not reflect dual group membership but instead communicates membership in the minority racial group. Therefore, the most difficult part of this task for individuals is the acceptance of black physical features, with this being more difficult for female respondents. Both Herring and Gibbs support this link between appearance and gender among their female biracial patients. Specifically, they both found that adolescent females were more likely to feel ashamed of and stigmatized by black physical traits.[28]

Whereas the previously mentioned studies found that appearance was important to the identity construction of biracial people, other research suggests that peers and family have more of an impact on identity construction than does physical appearance. Analyzing data from interviews with fourteen biracial respondents, Kerry Ann Rockquemore found no direct link between the physical appearance of her respondents and their racial identity.[29] Instead, parental socialization and peer influences proved to be more influential.

Contextual Factors and Identity

In addition to psychological adjustment, intergroup relations, and appearance, a small number of the studies we reviewed focused on the idea that racial identity is defined by an individual's social context. Social scientists, generally speaking, believe that individuals develop a sense of self and place in relation to those around them and their interactions with others. Although social context is an important issue to consider given the social construction of race, few studies have considered how contextual factors influence the development of racial identity within the biracial population. Some empirical evidence supports the assertion that racial identity among biracial people may vary according to context; yet, little research exists measuring the effects of presumably important contextual variables such as neighborhood or community composition and/or socioeconomic differences on racial identity development.[30]

At the micro level, one type of contextual factor—familial influence—was explored in three of the studies we reviewed. Bowles's study of ten biracial clinical patients found that families communicate subtle and explicit messages to children about their racial identity.[31] What families communicate to children regarding the identity they should adopt, she asserts, affects the children greatly. Her clinical findings are supported by a qualitative study of biracial adolescents by Christine Kerwin, Joseph Ponterotto, Barbara Jackson, and Abigail Harris, who conducted in-depth interviews with nine biracial people in the metropolitan New York City area. They found that familial influence was an important factor influencing the racial identity of their respondents. Biracial people whose families talked about racial issues openly were more likely to choose biracial as their self-definition and to be able to articulate strengths and weaknesses about being from an interracial family.[32]

Peer influence has also been found to be an important factor in the racial identity development of biracial people. Herring found that because conformity is expected and valued in adolescence, biracial teens may be rejected by both majority and minority peer groups, or as Gibbs reiterates, they may have difficulty with peers because they are "neither fish nor fowl."[33] The study conducted by Kerwin and her colleagues supported the importance of peer influence on racial identity construction among biracial adolescents, albeit in a nonclinical sample.[34] They found that adolescents could and did recall uncomfortable experiences of having to choose association with white or black peers. In addition, Bowles found that young adults in her sample felt marginalized and unaccepted not only by the racial group with which they identified but by either racial group.[35]

Racial Identity Development

Developmental models assume that the central task of adolescence is to form a stable identity. Some researchers using this theoretical frame suggest that biracials must successfully integrate dual racial and/or cultural identifications while also learning how to develop a positive self-concept and sense of competence. They also must develop the ability to synthesize their earlier identifications into a coherent and stable sense of a personal identity as well as a positive racial identity.[36] Others using the developmental model assume that the healthy racial identity for biracials is a black identity.[37]

Researchers working within a developmental framework all report negative findings for biracial adolescents. Gibbs and Herring suggest that the potential developmental problems facing biracial adolescents are numerous and arise when individuals experience conflicts in their efforts to resolve basic developmental tasks.[38] The problems they report include anxiety about social acceptance, rejection by peer groups, feelings of shame over physical appearance, rejection of one culture entirely, internalization of negative stereotypes, confusion over sexuality and partner choice, difficulty with separation from parents, and anxiety over career options.

The list of negative findings concerning biracial people's identity development is extensive. Biracial respondents have been found to have intense difficulty with racial identity formation, separation (as it implies rejection of one parent's race), relationship with the minority parent, and sexual identity development.[39]

Research based on stage theories of identity remains exploratory. This area of work would be greatly enhanced by longitudinal and comparative cross-sectional studies to ascertain the empirical validity of these theoretical ideals as they pertain to biracial subjects. Promising developments include the theoretical extension of developmental models to address the unique status of biracials.[40] These models, however, remain untested outside of clinical samples.[41]

Patterns and Limitations

Assessing the empirical literature as a whole, several patterns and limitations emerge. First and foremost, there is no consistency among existing studies in theory, method, or findings. This leads us to conclude that the field of empirical biracial research can best be described as a collection of disparate researchers operating independently from and seemingly unaware of one another. These various pieces lead to contradictory findings on the most basic questions about biracial identity construction and maintenance.

The methodological limitations of the studies we reviewed are also highly problematic. The sample sizes in the studies ranged from four to forty respondents, making generalizations difficult. In fact, much of the pathology found by researchers can be explained by the fact that many studies generalize from a sample of clinical patients who differ significantly from a nonclinical population. Studies where interviews and surveys were conducted on nonclinical samples consistently drew respondents from snowball sampling of multiracial organizations on West Coast college campuses. This technique is equally constraining because it provides a small self-selective pool of respondents with similar attitudes and experiences.

Research Design

To delve more deeply into the social processes that govern the meaning of racial identity for black/white biracials and to overcome the previously mentioned methodological limitations, we collected data using a multiphase approach that included both qualitative and quantitative methods. Phase 1 of the research plan involved in-depth interviews with biracial undergraduates at an institution in the Midwest we'll call "Catholic University."[42] The interview study provided a framework from which a survey was produced and distributed in Phase 2 of the study. Respondents for the second phase were drawn from our so-called "Metro Community College" and "Urban University" in the Detroit metropolitan area. Results from the survey were then clarified in Phase 3 of the project through purposive interviewing of selected survey respondents.

Measuring racial identity has never been an exact science. The difficulty is only compounded when attempting to measure biracial identity. In this final section, we outline each phase of the research design employed in this study. The obstacles were many, and we address them, as well as our attempted methodological solutions, in each phase of data collection. The goal of this lengthy description is to provide enough detail to enable other researchers interested in studying the biracial population to be able to replicate and, we hope, improve on our research design.

It should be clarified at this point that the intent of our study was exploratory in nature. The purpose was not to test formal hypotheses but to generate an understanding about a growing and elusive population.[43] Therefore, our goals were to investigate a little-understood phenomenon through the collection of descriptive data, to identify important factors that may influence an individual's choice of racial identities, and to formulate a tentative explanatory model of the relationship between these factors and an individual's racial self-understanding.[44] A multimethod approach was used to collect data to facilitate these exploratory goals.

Phase 1: In-Depth Interviews

The Sample

In efforts to collect data on biracial people, researchers have run into numerous difficulties, including accurate identification of potential respondents and the ability to attract enough respondents to draw meaningful generalizations. Numerous data sets have been collected in the past five years; however, no published empirical studies have compiled samples exceeding forty black/white biracial respondents, and most studies have included, within a small nonrandom sample, respondents with varying combinations of racial backgrounds. The most often-cited research anthology of mixed-race people is Maria P. Root's *The Multiracial Experience: Racial Borders as the New Frontier.*[45] Although it is generally considered the most comprehensive collection of research on the biracial population, the largest sample used in any of the studies included in the anthology has thirty-one respondents. In fact, most of the studies in this text generalize broadly from anecdotal, biographical, or small interview studies of less than twenty respondents. Small samples that include large degrees of variance on elements as fundamental as racial/ethnic combination of parents make it extremely difficult to draw any meaningful generalizations whatsoever. The first phase of data collection attempted to develop a unique solution to the problem of identifying potential respondents. Collecting survey data in Phase 2 of the research design addressed the need to have a large enough sample to detect patterned attitudes and behavior.

In the first phase of the research design, we conducted in-depth interviews with biracial undergraduates at Catholic University, a private Catholic university in the Midwest. The selection criterion was that respondents must have one black-identifying biological parent and one white-identifying biological parent. Our intention was to collect qualitative data for descriptive analysis. These data were also used to create the survey instrument for Phase 2 of the research design. All students registered as black or African American at the university were contacted. This list was generated from the university registrar and provided by the African American Studies Department. A solicitation for participation in the study was e-mailed to each of the 221 students who registered as black. Fourteen of the students responded that they fit the selection criteria and were willing to participate in the study; they were interviewed.

The Interviews

The fourteen students who responded to our call for participation ranged in age from 18 to 22 and were raised in ten different states in the United States. The students were uniformly affluent, and all came from families in which at least one parent had completed a bachelor's degree. The interviews took place at a variety of locations on the campus of Catholic University, including the dining hall, the coffee shop, the food court, and the lounge of the student union. Each of the interviews took place in a public setting and lasted between one and three hours. The average interview was one hour and thirty minutes long. All interviews were audiotaped and transcribed by a third party.

The interview guide consisted not of structured questions and answers but of general predefined topic areas. These were designed to guide the interviews in a loosely structured manner. The general topic areas included descriptions of experiences growing up, schooling (elementary through high school), friendships, significant others, transitions to college, descriptions of interactions with strangers, and self-perceptions. Appendix A contains a complete set of guidelines used for the interviews. In addition, each respondent signed a Consent Form (Appendix B) at the beginning of the interview, reacted to the "Bill of Rights for Racially Mixed People" (Appendix C), and filled out a one-page demographic questionnaire (Appendix D); each respondent's picture was taken.[46]

Phase 2: Mail Survey

The Sample

The selection criterion for the second phase of data collection was the same as the first: Respondents had to have one black-identifying biological parent and one white-identifying biological parent. Given the specified criterion, we drew respondents from two educational institutions in Detroit, Michigan: Urban University and Metro Community College. By collecting a sample from two Detroit area schools, we hoped to include individuals who would be comparable along the dimension of education level, purposively stratified by socioeconomic indicators, yet varied in appearance and identity. The sample we obtained from Catholic University (in Phase 1) was severely limited because students were homogeneous in social network composition, age, and life experience and highly skewed in socioeconomic status.

Urban University is a large private university enrolling about 4,600 students, 30 percent of them African American. Yearly tuition was $13,350, with room and board costing an additional $4,930. Metro Community College, in contrast, is a district-supported institution that has an open enrollment policy and about 21,000 students. Students come to this suburban campus from both the city of Detroit and the suburbs. Black students make up about 15 percent of the overall student population, and most commute to the institution from the city of Detroit. Tuition costs district residents $1,470 per year and out-of-district residents $2,200 per year. Drawing respondents from these two distinct educational institutions accomplished the sampling goals of building in variance along important sociodemographic characteristics while correcting some of the limitations encountered in Phase 1.

A request for participation in the study (Appendix E) was mailed to 4,532 students registered as black or African American, "Other," or those who left the race question blank. The rationale for this decision was drawn from the sampling strategy used at Catholic University, where e-mail solicitation of African American students supplied the initial biracial respondents. The Phase 1 interviews revealed that even students who most militantly stated in the interviews that they were biracial (i.e., they were "*not* black") indicated they had identified as black or African American on their college admission forms. This was done for two reasons: (a) the desire for social or organizational inclusion and (b) perceived individual gain. Students stated that they "checked the black box" instead of "other" (and writing in biracial or mixed) because they did not want to be excluded from activities that were targeted for the black student population, such as solicitations for black student organizations or announcements of special speakers. The second and more salient reason was that students felt that "it couldn't hurt" their opportunities for admission or for financial aid, which may be designated for minority students. Given this consistent response, soliciting the entire black student population at each institution seemed to be the most efficient way to draw out a group of biracial respondents. The limitation of the Phase 1 sampling strategy was that we potentially missed individuals with one black and one white parent who identified as white. To attempt to compensate for this shortcoming, we included individuals who had registered as Other and those who left the race question blank on their admissions forms. Although this may not have resolved the issue entirely, we were able to get considerably more variance among respondents from Metro Community College and Urban University than we did from the Catholic University sample.

A sample of college students was used primarily to control for education among respondents. It seemed necessary to try to maintain some level of consistency within the sample on selected factors while allowing for other, more salient factors to vary. The Detroit metropolitan area was selected because of its large African American population, diversity of neighborhoods and social contexts, and high degree of residential segregation. Both the community college and the private university enroll students from all parts of the metropolitan area, allowing for respondents who live both inside and outside the racially homogeneous city limits. Both institutions have students who range in age, socioeconomic status, and life experience, all of which were factors examined in the process of the research project. Despite the restriction of the sample to college students, we found a large amount of variance among our respondents. They ranged in age from 18 to 58 (the average age was 25); were 60 percent female and 40 percent male; came from low, middle, and upper middle class backgrounds; and had various physical appearances.

The Survey

The Survey of Biracial Experiences (Appendix F) was eleven pages in length and consisted of 102 open- and closed-ended questions. The survey questions were developed from analysis of in-depth interview data collected in Phase 1 of the research process. The survey was then pretested on all African American students at Catholic University, with an 82 percent response rate. Numerous corrections and adjustments were made based on the comments and responses of pretest respondents. The finalized survey was approved by all of the participating institutions.[47]

Following the distribution of 4,532 letters requesting participation in the study from students at Metro Community College and the Urban University, we received about 5 percent reply cards indicating a willingness to complete a survey. The finalized surveys were promptly mailed to respondents along with a brief explanatory cover letter and a postage-paid envelope. About 85 percent of the surveys were returned. Some respondents had not read the solicitation carefully and realized they did not fit the selection criteria once they received the survey in the mail. Those respondents called to inform us, returned the survey with a note stating the reasons for its return, or simply did not return the survey.

Two-hundred-fifty individuals responded to the initial solicitation and were surveyed. After cleaning the data and removing cases with missing data, cases in which the non-black parent was any race other than white, and those cases where the biracial individual was adopted, we were left with 177 cases for our analyses. The fact that we retained 177 cases out of 4,532 respondents may be interpreted in several ways. First and foremost, it may be the case that only a very small number of individuals fit the selection criteria (i.e., there are very few students with one black and one white parent among those registered at the two institutions). A second possible interpretation is that only a small number of individuals wish to participate in a survey of any kind, irrespective of whether or not they fit the sample criteria. Finally, it is also possible that individuals who have one black and one white parent registered for college either using a category other than black or Other or leaving the race question blank.[48]

Phase 3: In-Depth Interviews

The Sample

The final phase of data collection occurred after all surveys had been collected and preliminary analysis had been completed. The final survey question had asked respondents if they would be willing to participate in an in-depth interview. If their answer to that question was yes, they were directed to provide contact information. We then purposively subsampled from the total group of respondents with the intention of interviewing representative individuals.

The Interviews

Semistructured, in-depth interviews were conducted with twenty-five respondents, where all had indicated a willingness to be interviewed. Each respondent completed a Consent Form (Appendix G), as in the Phase 1 interviews. We began each interview by asking respondents what their racial identity was, and then we asked questions to ascertain why they answered the way they did. The questions inquired about the racial composition of the respondent's social networks, early childhood experiences, interactions with different racial groups, parental socialization, experiences of discrimination, and group evaluations of both blacks and whites.

Limitations

There are well-known problems in engaging a sample of biracial respondents.[49] The primary dilemmas are (a) the difficulty in identifying potential respondents and (b) the sensitive nature of the subject matter. We addressed the difficulty in identifying potential respondents by soliciting individuals from the population of students at the educational institutions who identified themselves on their admissions forms as African American or Other or provided no racial information.

It is possible that our selection strategy may omit biracial people who identify as white. However, we think this concern is mitigated by the fact that most biracial individuals in Phase 1 interviews stated that they identified as black on their college applications as a rational choice to provide a perceived advantage in the college admissions process. In addition, there is no support in the existing literature on biracial identity, the historical research on racial identity, or the current normative system of racial categorization to support an assumption that individuals with one black and one white parent would identify themselves as white. Although we may have omitted cases that exist due to our sampling strategy, we did not find compelling empirical justification to expect that *white* is a frequent identity choice made by black/white biracial people.

The data collected are used in the following chapters to explore the meaning of biracial identity in the United States and the factors that influence why black/white biracial individuals have very different understandings of their racial identity. The data provide a window into how biracial people construct and maintain their racial identities in the unique historical context of post-civil rights America. The survey data provide part of the overall picture and allow for some degree of theoretical generalization, whereas interview data contribute the richer detail about how and why biracial people develop their unique understandings of what it means to be biracial.

3

What Does Biracial Identity Mean?

In the introductory chapter, we highlighted the recent public debate concerning modifications to the 2000 census. Proponents have argued that the dramatic increases in interracial marriages over the past three decades have caused a "biracial baby boom."[1] This expanding population of biracial Americans, advocates argue, should be recognized by the government as multiracial. Those who opposed the possible addition of a multiracial category argued quite the opposite. From their perspective, biracial Americans are still viewed by society as black and, therefore, they develop a self-understanding of their racial identity as members of the black community.

We suggested that this debate was the latest litmus test for the one-drop rule as the official norm for answering the question, Who is black? in the United States. Children of black/white marriages have historically been considered part of the African American community; however, multiracial advocates have proposed an alternative response through their quest for separate group recognition. By demanding an independent governmental designation for mixed-race people, they are, in fact, arguing for nullification of the one-drop rule.

Critical to the arguments on both sides of the census debate are contrasting and mutually exclusive visions of how mixed-race people understand their racial identity. Multiracial advocates suggest the category is necessary as an accurate reflection of the way that biracial people self-identify. Opponents of the measure hold steadfast that biracial people experience the world and their place in it as African Americans. This chapter focuses on the tension between the rhetoric of political lobbyists and the broad and complex reality of individuals' experiences. We present the findings of our descriptive data analysis to address the questions at the heart of this debate. What does it mean to be biracial according to members of this population? Is there a singular way in which people with one black and one white parent understand their racial identity, or does biracial have multiple meanings?

Theoretical Framework of Identity Formation

Our conceptual framework rests on the three classic assumptions of symbolic interactionism: (a) that people know things by their meanings, (b) that meanings are created through social interaction, and (c) that meanings change through interaction.[2] Given these basic assumptions, it is necessary to clearly delineate the conceptual terminology used in the following discussion. First and foremost, what do we mean by the term *identity*?

Social actors are situated within societies that designate available categories of identification, how these identities are defined, and their relative importance. The term *identity* refers to a validated self-understanding that places and defines the individual; it establishes what and where an actor is socially.[3] *What* means in terms of the universal categories of signification that allow others to understand us, us to understand them, and us to understand ourselves (however misplaced these understandings may be). *Where* refers to the place within the social structure that an individual holds. Both of these are processes by which individuals understand themselves and others, as well as evaluate their self in relation to others. Identity is the direct result of mutual identification through social interaction. It is within this process of validation that identity becomes a meaning of the self.[4] Therefore, we use the term *identity* interchangeably with self-understanding throughout our discussion of the data analysis.

By situating identity within an interactionist framework, we understand biracial identity as an emergent category of identification. If identity is conceptualized as an interactionally validated self-understanding, then identities can only function effectively where the response of individuals to themselves (as social objects) is consistent with the response of others. In this schema, individuals cannot effectively possess an identity that is not socially typified; there must be no disjuncture between the identity actors appropriate for themselves and the place others assign to them as a social object. In other words, an individual cannot have a realized identity without others who validate that identity. The challenge of research on biracial identity, then, is twofold. First, we must explore how individuals understand their social location as biracial, and second, we must examine the social and interactional factors that lead to the development of this identity and the ways individuals try to realize their appropriated identities in social context. This chapter focuses on the first of these challenges.

Biracial Identity

What does biracial identity mean according to members of this population? Because we conceptualize the term identity to mean an interactionally validated self-understanding, another way of formulating the question becomes how do individuals interpret their biracialism and respond to it? Our data suggest some tentative descriptive categories for the ways that black/white multiracial people understand their biracialism: (a) a border identity, (b) a singular identity, (c) a protean identity, and/or (d) a transcendent identity. These categories of self-understanding are not necessarily mutually exclusive; rather, they should be viewed as ideal types. Each of these different interpretations of biracial identity is explored and discussed in the context of the data collected.

A Border Identity

Anthony was a six-foot tall, 18-year-old college football player.[5] His appearance can be best described as ambiguous; it would be difficult for anyone to guess his racial background, although he does not appear white. Anthony was raised in a small rural community in northern Ohio. His father (black) left his mother (white) when Anthony and his brother were young; therefore, they were raised exclusively by their mother and her extended family. There was a deep sense of tangible resentment when Anthony spoke about his father and a self-satisfied revenge that he and his brother had become successful, despite their abandonment.

Anthony was popular in his high school and reported attending a school with several other self-identified biracial students. His hometown was predominately white; however, half of the non-white students in his high school were mixed-race. This accessible group of peers and their location in a predominately white setting helped account for the fact that Anthony had a very strong identity as biracial. When asked, he told me, "I'm *not* black, I'm biracial," with such a forceful expression that I could not doubt the seriousness of his conviction. Anthony told numerous stories about incidents in high school where biracial students boldly differentiated themselves from black students by teasing them about the darkness of their skin. They affectionately referred to themselves as the "high yelluhs."

Gloria Anzaldua conceptualizes biracial identity as a border identity, one that lies between predefined social categories.[6] In essence, the border identity highlights an individual's existence between two socially distinct races as defining one's biracialism. Meaning lies in their location of in-betweenness, and this unique status serves to ground their racial identity. Mixed-race people who understand being biracial as a border identity don't consider themselves to be either black or white but, instead, incorporate both blackness and whiteness into a unique hybrid category of self-reference. One respondent explained that it was not only being on the border of socially defined categories but also experiencing the border status itself that brought with it an additional dimension:

> It's not that just being biracial is like you're two parts [white and black], you know, you have two parts but then there is also the one part of being biracial where you sit on the fence. There's a third thing, a unique thing.

The idea of a border identity has been the focus of numerous studies over the past 20 years.[7] In addition, a significant line of research has focused on developmental models of racial identity formation among biracials, where the border identity is the underlying ideal.[8] Christine Hall, studying black-Asian biracials, states that her adult respondents had all achieved a "multicultural existence," and they identified exclusively as biracial.[9] Barbara Tizard and Ann Phoenix found that 49 percent of their biracial British sample identified themselves as mixed-race and used terms such as *half-and-half, mixed,* or *brown.*[10] G. Reginald Daniel calls this identity a "blended identity" and describes it as one that "resists both the dichotomization and hierarchical valuation of African American and European American cultural and racial differences."[11]

A border identity is the most common way of conceptualizing biracialism among contemporary researchers focusing on the biracial population.[12] It can be inferred from most recent work that focuses on biracial people that when the term *biracial identity* is used it is being understood as a border identity. In addition, this conceptualization of biracial was most privileged by multiracial advocates in their quest for the addition of a multiracial category to the 2000 census.

In our sample, the border interpretation was the most common category of self-understanding. About 58 percent of those surveyed defined their racial identity as neither exclusively black nor white but, instead, as a third and separate category that draws from both of these group characteristics and has some additional uniqueness in its combination. It is important to note that these individuals fell into two distinguishable kinds of border identities: (a) those that are validated by others through social interactions (the validated border identity) and (b) those that are not (the unvalidated border identity). The importance of this distinction cannot be understated.

The Validated Versus Unvalidated Border Identity (the Real Tragic Mulattos?)

Chris was a calm woman who displayed a level of maturity beyond her years. Most people would assume that she is African American based on her appearance; however, she described her identity as "biracial, but I experience the world as a black woman." She talked freely about both her black and white extended families, recalling fond memories of the uniqueness of growing up in a loving family that was a patchwork of traditional black and Irish influences. However, she was acutely cognizant of how others viewed her, both strangers and those in her intimate social network.

Chris told me that because of her appearance race functioned as the first thing that many people saw about her and that many of the other roles that she played at school and in society were differentiated by her race. She was seen by others as the "*black* intern," a "*black* feminist," "a *black* student," and "a *black* friend." She expressed a close affiliation to other African Americans based on a common life experience of negotiating interactions as a person of color within a predominantly white culture. She felt that those close to her appreciated and understood her as biracial, but when she had to interact with people outside of her immediate social network, they categorized her as black, attributing to her all the assumptions and pre-conceived ideas that go along with that particular racial group member-ship. This made her feel both sad and somewhat resigned to the fact that there would always be a chasm between her self-identification (as biracial) and society's identification of her (as black).

For about 20 percent of the total respondents, their racial identity was exclusively biracial and that identity was validated by others. They described their racial identity in the following way: "I consider myself exclusively as biracial (neither black nor white)." However, more than 38 percent of respondents answered, "I consider myself biracial, but I experience the world as a black person." This is of interest because whereas 58 percent of *all* our respondents identified themselves as bira-cial (as opposed to exclusively black or white), more than half of that group expressed a disjuncture between their self-understanding and the way in which they socially experienced race. The difference between these two sets of responses seems to suggest the importance of interactional validation, which can best be understood by unpacking this second, unvalidated response.

Interviews with people like Chris offer additional insight into the un-validated border identity. Although she views herself as biracial, the social world fails to validate her chosen category of self-understanding. Given both the consistency and frequency of this nonvalidation, she lives in a gray area between her own self-understanding and the differential view that others have of her. She may consider herself biracial, being neither black nor white but something that lies uniquely in between. She qualifies this, however, with the honest recognition that she "experiences the world as a black person," meaning that within her social context her self-understanding of being biracial is not always validated by others. Consistent with this self-understanding/validation split is the fact that when asked about dif-ferent arenas of identity expression, respondents in the unvalidated border group were more likely to report their cultural, political, physical, and bureaucratic identity (i.e., the identity they select on forms) as black than as biracial.

If these univalidated border individuals, as social actors, appropriate an identity for themselves as biracial, then why do others fail to place them as a social object into the same category? There seem to be two logical possibilities to answer that question. First, others may not understand biracial as an existing category of racial classification, so they may be operating with only the dichotomous, mutually exclusive categories black and white. This is the very situation that the multiracial movement is attempting to address. The second possible explanation for this classification failure is that even if others possess cognitive categories for black, white, and biracial, the individual's appearance may be composed of characteristics that would lead others to nonetheless classify them as black. Although the first explanation is certainly a viable possibility, we are unable to explore it with the existing data. The second explanation, however, led us to examine the differences between the self-reported appearance of the validated and unvalidated border identities (see Chapter 5).

Finally, it may be asked how individuals could develop a racial identity that is unvalidated if identity itself has been conceptually defined as an interactionally validated self-understanding. In other words, how can the unvalidated border identity be developed and maintained if others do not recognize its existence? We need only return to Chris to see that, in reality, her identity as biracial is validated by her significant others, such as her parents and friends. At the primary level of social intimacy, she feels that her authentic self is validated and realized. It is in the more everyday, nonintimate social meetings with strangers and acquaintances that she is unvalidated and routinely misidentified. We have parenthetically referred to the unvalidated border identity as the real "tragic mulattos" because it is precisely this group that experiences an internalized social dislocation because of its continual oscillation between having its self-understanding validated by some and unvalidated by others. The clinical and therapeutic literature focusing on biracial identity has primarily dealt with the group of black/white biracials whom we refer to as unvalidated borders.[13]

A Singular Identity

John looked white. When he first walked into my classroom, I unconsciously had him categorized as a "typical white fraternity guy."[14] He was medium height, in his early twenties, and quiet. The fact that he was biracial didn't surface until much later in the course when another student was presenting a project. He volunteered the fact that his mother (white) had been raped by a black man and had twins, a sibling who died in the hospital and himself. John was raised in an affluent, exclusively white community.

He had a highly strained relationship with his stepfather, who had not revealed the circumstances of his conception and birth to John until he was 18 years old.

John had lived his entire life assuming that he was white, that he came from a white family, and that his stepfather was his biological father, despite the fact that they had no physical similarities. When John was a teenager, he was told that his lips and nose were a bit wide for the modeling career he envisioned, so he had plastic surgery to thin his lips and trim his nose. His identity as white was entirely unaffected by the sudden revelation that his biological father was black. It didn't cause him to rethink his identity nor to question his whiteness. He was simply a white man who happened to have a black father.

John illustrates the racial identity option of individuals with one black and one white parent, an option that we term the *singular identity*. In the singular understanding, the individual's racial identity is exclusively either black or white. Being biracial means merely acknowledging the racial categorization of a person's birth parents. At the extreme, respondents did not deny the existence of their opposite race parent, but it was not salient in defining their self-understanding and may not have been offered as identifying information unless specifically requested.

Researchers, past and present, have unquestionably considered this identity option, given that the singular black identity has been the historical norm. Maria Root suggested the singular identity as one (of several) resolutions of "Other Status," proposing that biracial individuals may choose to identify with a single racial group.[15] This identity option encompasses both the singular black and singular white options. However, Root narrowed the parameters for the singular white option by asserting geographic specificity (i.e., this option is not available in the South), thus emphasizing the importance of sociocultural context and the racial composition of a biracial individual's socialization networks. The singular black identity is characterized by Root as the biracial person "accepting the identity that society assigns."[16] This identity option has been heavily studied and is still assumed to be the primary option for black/white biracial individuals. Interestingly, the singular identity was highly contested in the census debate. Whereas African Americans emphasized this identity option as the identity choice of black/white biracials, many multiracial activists doubted the very existence of the singular black identity. Both sides in the census debate, however, fell silent on the possibility of a singular white identity.

About 13 percent of our sample considered themselves "exclusively black (or African American)," and almost 4 percent of the sample considered themselves "exclusively white (not black or biracial)." Given the centrality of the assumption that the one-drop rule would dictate most directly how biracial individuals would racially self-identify, some may find it surprising that such a small number of the respondents chose the singular black identity. This finding illustrates the complex nature of racial identity among biracial people in the United States, a complexity that is further explored in Chapters 4 and 5.

A Protean Identity

Mike was a gregarious and enjoyable individual. He was a popular student at the university and seemed to know almost everyone who walked into the coffee shop on the evening of our interview. Mike had finished college when we interviewed and was completing a semester of student teaching at a local public high school. Mike was raised in a small town in the Midwest. His parents were the only interracial couple in the area. In fact, they were such an anomaly that he had a newspaper clipping in which his parents were featured on the front page. Mike's father was a minister in the local church, which afforded his family a uniquely high and visible status in their community.

Although Mike was the only non-white person in his neighborhood, school, and friendship circle, he had close ties with his black extended family, whom he saw on a regular basis. Mike thought that it was his particular upbringing that led him to view his racial identity as he now understands it, which he describes as changing and shifting according to the group of people that he is with and the social context. The lesson he has learned from being around homogeneous groups of blacks and whites his entire life is that there are different ways of being in a group of blacks versus a group of whites.

Although many people might agree with this idea, regardless of their race, Mike's version is a bit different from most. Not only does he realize that these situations require different social behaviors, but he has the unique experience of feeling more than knowledgeable about these different behaviors, sensing that when he is in these groups, he is accepted by members of the group as an insider. Although most people might adjust their *behavior* to differing circumstances, Mike adjusts his *identity* to these different circumstances. He feels that he has the capacity to understand himself as black when he is with blacks and that his self-understanding is fully validated. He feels that he is able to understand himself as white when he is with whites and that this self-understanding is fully validated.

Furthermore, he feels that he is able to understand himself as biracial when he is in a heterogeneous group, and that self-understanding is also validated. For Mike, any social situation must be assessed for what identity will "work," and then that particular identity is presented. Is this shape shifting viewed as problematic for him? On the contrary, he views his ability effectively to possess, present, and have different identities accepted as authentic by different groups of people as the "gift of being biracial."

Respondents like Mike understand biracial identity as their protean capacity to move among cultural contexts.[17] Their self-understanding of biracialism is directly tied to their ability to cross boundaries between black, white, and biracial, which is possible because they possess black, white, and biracial identities. These individuals feel endowed with a degree of cultural savvy in several social worlds and understand biracialism as the way in which they are accepted, however conditionally, in varied interactional settings. They believe their dual experiences with both whites and blacks have given them the ability to shift their identity according to the context of any particular interaction. This contextual shifting leads individuals to form a belief that their multiple racial backgrounds are but one piece of a complex self composed of assorted identifications that are not culturally integrated. When the topic of racial identification was initially broached with Mike, he said, "Well, shit, it depends on what day it is and where I'm goin'."

The understanding of biracialism as the ability to be black, white, and/or biracial in different contexts has been discussed by several multiracial researchers.[18] Root, although not using the term *protean*, briefly discussed this option as one where individuals have "fluidity"; however, she says no more and does not separate these individuals out as any different from the border/biracial option.[19] In her later work, Root describes these individuals as having "both feet in both groups."[20] Both Root and Cookie Stephan have depicted this shifting as practicing "situational race."[21] Daniel alluded to the protean option when he discussed those who had an "Integrative Identity," individuals who reference themselves *simultaneously* in black and white communities.[22] This is different from the border identity, in that those individuals typically seek biracial communities and networks. Daniel makes a further distinction into two subtypes: (a) a synthesized integrative identity, where individuals feel equally comfortable in both black and white cultural settings; and (b) a functional integrative identity, where individuals are able to identify and function in both communities but feel a stronger orientation to, acceptance in, and comfort with either blacks or whites. Empirically, Tizard and Phoenix's study of mixed-race individuals in Great Britain found that 10 percent of respondents said they were black "in some situations," whereas another 10 percent felt they were white "in some situations."[23] Robin Miller also briefly mentions that it is probable that many biracials have fluid identities that adjust to their surroundings and social contexts.[24]

Understanding biracialism as a protean identity was the least frequent choice made by the mixed-race people we surveyed. Only 4 percent of the respondents selected this option when asked about their identity. Despite the small number of our respondents who chose this identity option, it is one that is of great theoretical interest, given the persistent self-monitoring of the actors' presentation of self and their purposive manipulation of appearance. This identity option is discussed in much greater detail in Chapters 4 and 5.

A Transcendent Identity

Rob was in his senior year of college when we arranged to meet in a coffee shop on campus. Typically, when I arrived, I could pick out my interviewee immediately. When I went to meet Rob, however, I couldn't tell who I was supposed to meet, because everyone in the coffee shop looked white. Finally, a tall young man came up to my table and asked if we were supposed to meet for an interview; he had been watching me look around for him all along. I told him immediately that he didn't look mixed, and he responded, "Neither do you. I just saw you looking around the room and figured you were the person I was supposed to meet." This first incident in our meeting is illustrative of our conversation about race and identity because it reveals both Rob's and my own construction of reality. Throughout our interview, I stayed locked in a social world that is perceived through the lens of race, and Rob consistently and repeatedly questioned my "fixation."

Rob was born and raised in a medium-size midwestern city. His parents were both teachers, and he had several brothers and sisters. He recalled growing up in an intellectually stimulating household, where parents and siblings were encouraged to read, write, and discuss political and social matters openly. Rob attended an integrated public school and found friendship within diverse circles. Rob was adamant that race was a false categorization of humanity and did not want to be thought of as a member of any racial category whatsoever. Rob's greatest desire was to be understood by others as the unique individual he was, to be appreciated for his particular gifts and talents, and not to be "pigeon-holed" into a preformulated category that carried with it a multitude of assumptions about the content of his character. Rob was not black, white, or biracial. He was a musician, a thinker, a kind-hearted individual, a good friend, a Catholic, and a hard-working student with dreams and ambitions. For Rob, race had interfered with others perceiving his authentic self, and he could see that it would continue to color how others viewed him, his work, and his personal talents in the future.

After conducting the first round of interviews, Rob was given a transcript of our interview and a draft of a conference paper that was in progress based on our data analysis. He contacted us shortly thereafter to ask if we could meet again. At that time, we had only conceptualized three of the identity options we ultimately determined (the border, singular, and protean identities). He confronted us with the fact that he didn't see himself in any of these categories and that he resented being either falsely stuffed into a rigid and unrepresentative typology or being excluded as an "outlying case." After a lengthy discussion, we were forced to rethink the initial grouping and added this additional type of understanding that race has for biracial individuals. We call this nonracial self-understanding the transcendent identity.

The literature on biracial identity has been remarkably silent on this option for black/white biracial individuals. The transcendent identity, as described here, is noteworthy because these individuals claim to opt out of the categorization game altogether. Only Daniel recognizes that being biracial could produce a transcendent understanding of the self when he argues that individuals who possess both "pluralistic" (neither black, white, nor necessarily biracial) and "integrative" (a blending of black and white) identities can display transcendent characteristics.[25] He suggests that the transcendent phenomenon is more likely to be found among biracial people who identify with and reference themselves in both white and black communities in roughly equal amounts than among those who feel more comfortable in the company of other mixed-race people.

After examining the survey data, it became clear that some individuals understood their biracialism as transcendent and similar to Robert Park's classic conception of the "marginal man."[26] In other words, their status as biracial provided them with the perspective of the stranger. They perceived their detached, outsiders' perspective as enabling them to objectively articulate the social meaning placed on race and discount it as a "master status" altogether. These individuals responded to questions about their identity with answers that were unrelated to their racial status, as in the following example:

> I'm just John, you know. I never thought this was such a big deal to be identified, I just figured I'm a good guy, just like me for that, you know. But, when I came here [to college], it was like I was almost forced to look at people as being white, black, Asian, or Hispanic. And so now, I'm still trying to go "I'm just John," but uh, you gotta be something.

This respondent later talked about "using" race (to benefit others as a mentor or role model) in a way that suggested it was not only a pliable category that a person could fit into at will but, more important, that it's reality was highly questionable. Slightly less than 13 percent of our total sample understood being biracial as a transcendent identity.[27]

The transcendent identity seems, at first glance, to negate the theoretical framework of identity construction that we have proposed. How can an individual exist in a racially stratified society and have a nonracial identity validated? However, a closer look at the social psychological processes involved in the construction of these individual's racial identities (or lack thereof) actually underscores the importance of validation as an indispensable mechanism of identity maintenance. If, in fact, individuals who have this self-understanding truly possess the perspective of the stranger, then validation is meaningless. In other words, if individuals perceive themselves to have no racial identity and consciously view the existing system of racial classification as biologically baseless, yet symbolically meaningful to other members of society, then their participation in that system is equally meaningless to their individual self-understanding. To be explicit, if there is no racial identity to be validated, then the lack of validation for that identity is meaningless. For our respondents, claiming an identity on a form is simply filling out a box, devoid of any reflection of their personal self-understanding. Experiences of discrimination, perceived from the standpoint of the stranger, neither reinforce nor negate their existing sense of self. Respondents who chose the transcendent identity seemed content to be at the periphery of a racially divided America, annoyed by the inconveniences yet playing their role when necessary.

Discussion

Many researchers and multiracial advocates have assumed that mixed-race people share a singular understanding of what biracial identity means. Specifically, contemporary researchers have assumed that biracial identity is equivalent to the border identity, treating it as an idea for which a conceptual definition is unnecessary. A common assumption is that members of this population hold a clear and unified understanding of what biracial identity means and how that term translates into a racial self-understanding and/or group affiliation.[28] Both the in-depth interviews and survey data suggest that this is a misguided assumption because what it means to be biracial is conceptually complex and varies among biracial respondents. In other words, an analysis of the data suggests there is no singular understanding among black/white mixed-race people as to what biracial identity means or how it translates into an individual self-understanding.

The voices of biracial people reveal that there are varying understandings of what biracial identity means to members of this emerging population. Individuals have not one but several ways in which they may interpret and respond to the circumstance of having one black and one white parent. These divergent self-understandings are grounded in differential experiences, varying biographies, and cross-cutting cultural contexts. Having established that biracial identity is multidimensional, the following chapters explore how individuals develop and maintain these very different self-understandings. Chapter 4 examines the influence of socialization factors on the choices that biracial individuals make about their racial identity, whereas Chapter 5 explores the effect of appearance.

4

Socialization and Biracial Identity

Mixed-race people make a variety of choices about their racial identity and the way that they understand what it means to be biracial in American society. Having described these various identity options in the previous chapter, we turn now to the important question of why individuals with one black and one white parent make radically different choices about their racial identity.

Choosing Between and Among Identity Options

Previous studies of racial and ethnic identity have attempted to specify both the socioeconomic and demographic determinants of people's group identity.[1] Mary Waters's work focused on ethnic options for individuals with multiple white-ethnic heritages.[2] Her primary interest was in why individuals with multiple ethnic backgrounds choose to emphasize one of their ethnicities over others. The factors that influenced choice among white ethnic options included (a) individuals' knowledge about an ethnicity, (b) their surname, (c) physical appearance, and (d) the general popularity of the ethnic groups among which they were choosing. Waters concluded that ethnicity was largely symbolic because it had no real consequences for an individual's life chances or everyday interactions. Fundamentally, white ethnic identity is characterized by the existence of choice. In other words, white ethnics can choose to assume their ethnic identity or not in any given circumstance.

Waters's findings are important to the study of biracialism because they underscore the symbolic basis of white ethnicity and explicitly differentiate it from racial identity. The symbolic ethnicity of whites differs from that of non-whites because race is neither situational nor meaningless. Therefore, compared to the case of white ethnicity, racial identity options either are nonexistent or function according to a different set of normative rules because racial and ethnic categories are socioculturally stratified. Waters's work implies that racial and ethnic identities develop through dissimilar social processes due to visibility, the capacity of individual choice, and a history of stratification based on racial group membership.

Waters's work provides a necessary component for understanding why biracial individuals choose different identity options. However, it must be augmented by a consideration of the existing research on the determinants of black identity. This conceptual fusion is essential because (a) biracial individuals have historically and traditionally been considered members of the African American community and (b) most racial identity research (as opposed to *ethnic* identity research) focuses on the black population. The research literature on racial identity conceptualizes identity to be a particular subunit of an individual's overall self-concept. Identities, in this sense, are simply "meanings a person attributes to the self as an object in a social situation or social role."[3] To be African American in American society means that an individual occupies a racially defined, albeit socially constructed, ascribed status. That status implies a variety of roles within the family, community, and society. These broader socially defined roles have significant social-psychological implications. One of the implications is that membership in a defined racial category is accompanied by a group identity.

Significant differences exist between ethnic and racial identity research. Where ethnic identity is viewed in the late twentieth century as optional or symbolic, racial identity is viewed as multifaceted and encompassing both the group and individual.[4] Specifically, black group identity is used to refer to "the feeling of closeness to similar others in ideas, feelings, and thoughts."[5] Others have rejected this singular understanding; they say black group identity is multidimensional, including both in-group factors, such as closeness to other blacks and black separatism, and reflexive factors, such as racial group evaluation.[6]

An additional distinction between ethnic and racial identity research is the level of analysis used for explanation. Researchers studying ethnic identity, due to its symbolic nature, focus on individual-level characteristics to explain why people choose one ethnic identity over another. Racial identity research, however, emphasizes that black identity emerged from the historical, demographic, and structural specificity of the American cultural context, necessitating a consideration of structural-level explanatory factors, which have included geographic location, education, social network structure, and socioeconomic status.[7] In other words, racial identity researchers assume without question that choice simply does not exist. Therefore, an African-descended individual is assumed to have a multidimensional black identity.[8] Individual factors are de-emphasized in favor of structural explanations because individuals do not choose whether or not to have a racial identity as black, although their feelings about group membership are free to vary.

When examining a biracial sample, both frameworks are salient. We have demonstrated in the previous chapter that some degree of racial identity choice is present among black/white biracials. Because people choose among black, white, and biracial identities, we draw heavily on Waters's framework outlining an explanation of white ethnic options for our explanatory model. The existence of various identity options should not, however, suggest to the reader that the matter of choice for black/white biracials is unlimited. The existence of real structural constraints requires a reliance on the body of research on racial identity in general and on African American identity specifically. By weaving these two frameworks together, we provide a foundation on which we may better understand the empirical link between the social structure in which people are embedded, the social interactions they experience within that structure, and the power of socialization to shape and maintain racial identities.

Factors Influencing Racial Identity Choice

We established in the previous chapter that biracial individuals make diverse choices about their racial identities. Several factors influence the choices that they make, including individual factors (such as physical appearance) and structural factors (such as socioeconomic status, social network composition, and racial socialization). Each of these factors will be discussed in turn.

Appearance

Appearance provides information about individuals that helps others to define the self as situated. This information enables others to know in advance what they expect of an actor and what the actor can expect of them.[9] Appearance provides the first, albeit socially constructed, information about an individual to others in the context of face-to-face interaction. People's appearance helps define their identity and allows them an embodied means to express their self-identification. It is in this process that identities are negotiated and either validated or contested.[10]

Physical appearance is critical in the discussion of racial identities because the logic of racial categorization hinges on the ability of individuals instantaneously to place another person based on physical cues. Phenotypic categorizations, as the source of racial identity, encompass skin color, hair texture, and facial features. These physical characteristics may also be considered as presenting an individual's identity to others. In other words, physical appearance not only communicates people's identity but also has a reflexive relationship with identity. Because phenotype is at the core of racial identity, skin color has been considered important to racial identity development among biracial people and is most commonly linked to the development of a singular black racial identity.[11] Researchers have proposed a commonsense link between skin color and racial categorization, suggesting that the darker skinned the biracial individual, the more likely he or she is to be classified as black by others and to adopt a singular black identity.[12]

In our initial in-depth interviews, we heard respondents speak about their appearance as both a personal and a social characteristic. On one hand, they were able to describe their own phenotypic features (such as skin color). On the other hand, they described their appearance in social terms, as how other people categorized them (i.e., people always assume I'm black).[13] By separating our understanding of appearance, at one level, to the observable and objective dimension of skin color and, on another, to respondents' understanding of how other people categorize them, we allow the space for these two items to either contradict or support each other as a reflection of their relationship in the lives of our respondents.

Biracial people exist in an American system of cultural coding that imposes a uniquely dichotomous black/non-black schema of racial identification. The result is that identity options may be constrained by appearance and/or one's appearance and identity may be incongruous. Because racial categories are defined by appearance, the logic and enactment of racial categorization becomes questionable if individuals cannot be easily identified on sight. Research by Maria Root, Kerry Ann Rockquemore, and Theresa Williams provides illustrations of the interactional ruptures that occur when appearance fails to match identity, both for the identifier and the identified.[14]

Those who have studied the relationship between appearance and the racial identity of biracials have noted the difficulty in achieving enough variation in physical characteristics to make any substantial conclusions.[15] Our data were uniquely able to address this ongoing difficulty in two ways. First and foremost, we considered two aspects of appearance: self-perceived skin color and others' social perceptions. Second, and more important, our sample had significant variation on both of these dimensions.[16]

Many people expect that those who have dark skin are more likely to choose an exclusively black identity, those who have light skin will be more likely to choose a biracial identity, and those who appear white will identify as white. This runs contrary to the logic expressed in much of the literature on the biracial population.[17] Root, however, states that those who investigate "multidimensional models of identity will not be perplexed that phenotype . . . do[es] not necessarily correlate with or reliably predict identity."[18] We found that skin color did not predict identity choice. However, socially perceived appearance emerged as an important and influential factor in determining what racial identity our respondents chose. Given the significant importance of appearance in racial identification, we will briefly mentioned them here; however, the following chapter is entirely devoted to exploration of how this complex factor influences racial identity choice among biracial people.

Social Networks

Numerous researchers have theorized that social network composition influences racial identity construction and maintenance among biracial individuals.[19] An individual's pre-adult and adult social networks may include a vast number of potentially significant others such as family members, neighbors, and peers, who influence the daily interactional work of shaping and defining a person's identity. Racially homogeneous neighborhoods, whether predominately black or white, may provide differential parameters and assessments of the racial identity options available to biracial individuals.

F. James Davis suggests that the black community has deeply internalized the one-drop rule.[20] As a reflection of the pervasiveness of this norm, it is common within many predominately black communities that individuals of all phenotypic variations, as well as biracial people, are considered black. Rockquemore found that biracial individuals socialized within predominately black social networks were more likely to choose an exclusively black identity because of this sense of inclusiveness.[21] In contrast, those socialized in predominately white networks were more likely to develop a border identity because it is both available (i.e., socially acceptable) and preferable to the singular black identity. Others propose that in either predominately white or integrated social networks, individuals may develop a border identity because of the availability of cultural translators, mediators, and models.[22]

Because identity is an ongoing interactional process, the racial composition of an actor's social networks provides only a broad description for understanding racial identity choices. What occurs within those networks and the type of interactions that individuals have in those settings affect their choices of racial identity. We conceptualize this as *push and pull factors* where individuals, located within particular types of social networks, may feel pulled toward one racial identity option because of positive experiences with one group or may feel pushed away from another racial identity because of negative experiences.[23] Push factors within social networks that influence racial identification may include experiencing negative treatment from blacks. This type of experience may push a biracial person away from adopting a singular black identity. In contrast, if biracial individuals have negative interactional experiences with whites, they may be pushed away from a border or singular white identity.

Another important social-psychological process that occurs within the parameters of individuals' social network and may influence their choice of racial identity is feelings of closeness to particular racial groups. Lynda

Field found that those who had more positive feelings about African Americans as a group were more likely to choose the singular black identity as their racial identity.[24] Her work suggests that when individuals interact in social networks composed predominately of one group of people, they tend to feel closer to that group. This closeness and familiarity may, in and of itself, exert pull factors on biracial individuals and thereby influence their identity choices.

Socialization Factors:
Childhood and Adult Socialization

Families provide a social context in which individuals develop a sense of self, values, and beliefs.[25] Parent-child interactions are ongoing, intense, and deeply integral to the interactional processes of identification, modeling, and role-playing. Children learn within the family context who they are in relation to themselves, their family, and others in society.[26] The socialization process, by definition, serves the purpose of transmitting norms and values from one generation to the next. For members of non-white racial groups, socialization extends itself to encompass the norms and values of the unique racial group, as well as interweaving the racial group membership into the child's understanding of who he or she is.[27] Although there is a wide body of research on the problems associated with racial socialization, particularly the problems of socializing biracial children, there is little discussion of how parents socialize children into racial identities and/or how important parental socialization is in the development of racial identity.[28]

Although the family may be the primary agent of socialization, it is not the sole source of socialization. Individuals interact with a multitude of others in their pre-adult social context. Specifically, their social network can have a wide variety of characteristics, one of which is its racial composition. Existing empirical research demonstrates that racial group identification can be affected negatively by interracial contact *if* the racial context exposes an individual to prejudiced communications and to out-group norms, values, and attitudes.[29] In addition, a person's awareness of ethnic group membership decreases as the group becomes less distinct within a particular social environment.[30] Therefore, racial group identity can be expected to be positively developed in homogeneous social contexts or in interracial contexts that are not characterized by prejudiced attitudes and behaviors. This distinction leads us to examine separately (a) interracial contact and (b) experiences of discrimination.

Although the relationship of racial identity and the racial composition of social networks has been documented in the literature on African Americans, some ambiguity exists concerning how this relationship applies to the biracial population, given that homogeneous social networks for interracial families would imply a network composed of other interracial families. What is unique, then, to the biracial population is the improbability that individuals would exist in a homogeneous social context. In other words, it is highly unlikely that any respondent in this study was raised in a social network composed predominately of interracial couples and biracial children. Because of the rarity of their circumstance, it can be inferred that interracial contact is a normative experience for interracial families and their biracial offspring.

Familial Context

The socioeconomic status of an individual's family is especially important to racial identity formation. Family resources structure an individual's social network by determining the parameters of social activity including neighborhoods and schools. These, in turn, affect the types of people with whom individuals may develop friendships and the norms, values, and attitudes to which they may be exposed.[31] According to the literature on social structure and personality, it could be expected that much of the effect of parents' social class on racial identity would be indirect, operating through the microsocial interaction processes such as parent socialization and interracial contact.[32]

A great deal of the existing literature on racial identity focuses on black children. Studies of adult racial group identification are much more limited. Socialization theory has a natural tendency to focus on individuals in the pre-adult stage, assuming that socialization is complete and racial identity is fully formed by the time an individual reaches adulthood. David Demo and Michael Hughes argue that it is imperative to question the degree to which adult social structure and social process variables affect black identity, independent of childhood background and socialization variables.[33] Researchers analyzing the life course provide ample evidence to support this relationship between adult roles and personality.[34] Certainly, adults have different cognitive capacities and reasoning abilities than children do; therefore, we would expect a different type of interaction to occur between their structural location and their racial identity maintenance.[35]

Numerous factors may be important as predictors of adult racial identity for African Americans. Research conducted by David Demo, Stephen Small, and Ritch Savin-Williams reveals that the quality of interpersonal relations with family and friends positively influences both racial self-esteem and feelings of closeness to other blacks.[36] Religious participation has also been explored as an important socializing factor because black churches have historically allowed African Americans to hold positions of authority unavailable in other social institutions, leading to increased self-respect, positive group evaluation, and enhanced psychological well-being.[37] Adult socioeconomic status has been shown in at least two studies to be negatively related to feelings of closeness to other blacks.[38] Finally, research focusing on adult interracial interaction has found that existence outside a racially homogeneous community minimizes black group identification.[39]

Based on a reading of the literature and our analysis of in-depth interviews, we created a conceptual model of the determinants of biracial identity choice among our respondents. We believed that appearance, social network structure, and socialization factors influenced identity construction. In the remaining section of this chapter, we present each of the four identity options to explore the interpretive power of these factors.

Biracial: A Border Identity

Mixed-race individuals make varying choices about their racial identity. One of those choices, the border identity, involves the creation of a new category of identification, one that encompasses both of the socially accepted racial categorizations of black and white yet includes an additional element from its combination. These respondents make up 58 percent of our total sample and can be further subdivided into those whose identity as biracial is validated versus those whose identity as biracial is unvalidated. The difference between those two subgroups lies in respondents' perception of the response that others have to their racial group membership. Both subgroups understand being biracial as a border identity. However, some have that identity validated by others in their social network, whereas others fail to have biracial accepted as a legitimate category of racial identification. This latter group of individuals answered the identity question by saying "I consider myself biracial, but I experience the world as a black person."

The primary individual-level factor that influences the racial identity choice of biracial people is physical appearance. The appearance variable is a self-report of the respondents' appearance, ranging from "I look black and most people assume that I am black" to "I physically look white, I could 'pass.'" Appearance is highly significant as a factor influencing the development of a validated border identity. Our data suggest that if an individual's physical appearance is closer to whites than to blacks, they are more likely to understand being biracial as a border identity, and this identity is more likely to be validated than unvalidated. For those whose appearance is closer to blacks than to whites, their identity as biracial is less likely to be validated. Chapter 5 provides a more extensive discussion of the role of appearance in racial identity construction.

It is too simplistic to say that biracial individuals' appearance alone determines their racial identity. The effect of social networks in which an individual is situated must also be considered to understand their identity choice. Individuals are socially located in systems of networks or social relationships that are directly related to their social status. Different status levels provide access to various types of social networks. For biracial individuals, the higher the status of their parents, the more likely that they will have contact with white peer groups. The more time that individuals spend interacting with white peers, the less likely they are to develop an understanding of their biracialism as a singular (black) identity. Specifically, the more time that individuals spend in white peer groups, the more likely they are to cultivate a degree of cultural savvy to fit in with these peers and to see both whiteness and blackness in their self-understanding and interactional presentation of self.

The racial compositions of the pre-adult and adult social networks of those possessing the validated and unvalidated border identity options are different from each other *and* different from the racial context of those choosing the singular black, protean, or transcendent identity. Choosing the validated border identity is correlated with having predominantly white pre-adult social networks, especially when compared to the other identity options. In contrast, those having an unvalidated border identity had many more African Americans in their pre-adult social networks than those choosing the validated border identity. On reaching adulthood, those with a validated border identity retain the racial composition of their social networks (i.e., which continue to be composed primarily of whites). However, for those who choose the unvalidated border identity, their shift from pre-adult to adult social networks is marked by a change in the racial composition of their social networks. Specifically, they undergo a change from predominantly black pre-adult networks to predominantly white adult networks. This racial composition change from pre-adult to adult social networks for unvalidated border biracials is greater than for all other identity groups and may be important in understanding why their racial identity fails to be validated by others.

The preceding statement suggests that it is merely access to different types of networks that influences racial identity development. It is important to note, however, that it is not merely the amount of contact an individual has with either white or black peers or family members, as suggested by Hall, nor is it exclusively which group the individual uses as a reference group, as suggested by Field.[40] Instead, it is the type of contact that individuals have with others, or the way in which they socially experience race, that mediates the relationship between their social status and their racial identity.

Respondents choosing the validated and unvalidated border options report the highest levels of negative interactions with blacks (as compared to respondents choosing the other identity options). Again, we must put this in the context of the racial composition of their social networks. The networks of those choosing a validated border identity tend to be predominately white in both their pre-adult and adult lives. Having few African Americans in their social network and experiencing negative treatment from those few people may serve as a push factor away from the development of a black identity and a pull factor toward the development of an exclusively biracial identity. For the unvalidated group, once again, there is a very different set of experiences. Their pre-adult social networks are populated by blacks, yet they report the most negative treatment from blacks. This context, although different from that of the validated border group, serves the same function—to push individuals away from the development of a singular black identity and pull them toward the border identity. When their networks change to predominately white, that pull is magnified.

Closeness to whites and blacks serves as a confirmatory measure of feelings of social distance between our respondents and these two different racial groups. Whereas respondents who identify themselves as exclusively black report feeling close to blacks and not close to whites, those who choose the validated border identity report feeling less close to blacks and closer to whites. The unvalidated border group, in comparison, feels as close to blacks as those respondents choosing the singular black identity, yet closer to whites than this group. The combination of existing in pre-adult social networks that are heavily populated with blacks, experiencing negative social interactions with blacks, and feeling closer to blacks than whites could explain the conflicted nature of the unvalidated border group. They experience negativity from both whites and blacks as they move from blacker contexts to whiter ones throughout their life cycle. This experience of both push and pull factors may explain the inherent tension in their racial identity.

The previously mentioned factors, when considered in the aggregate, help provide a broad picture of biracial people who choose the border identity. An additional case from the in-depth interviews illustrates, in a more tangible way, how social networks create the context for identity development. Kathy is a biracial woman from New York. She is white in appearance, with fair skin, long, curly, light brown hair, freckles, and green eyes. She attended public schools, in which the student population was about 50 percent black, until the tenth grade. She stated the following in reference to her relationships with black students:

I was always rejected by the black women. I just shied away from the black males because they were a little intimidating and a little too aggressive, I thought. So then when I transferred sophomore year, I went to a Catholic school that only had maybe about ten blacks counting the four biracial students so when I got there I was really taken in by these people and it was just a total different world. It was like [in public school] I was really never accepted by these black females because well, you [referring to the interviewer] probably been told this too, they were jealous because you have good hair and light eyes. I remember thinking what were they jealous of? I didn't choose to be like this, I don't mind it, you know what I mean, so it was really their problem I think. Then I went to Catholic school. . . . I didn't really know anybody, and I was just like hopefully, it will be better. Of course, it was better because there was less black people for me to contend with. . . . Maybe because it was a Catholic prep school that was $4,000 a year, that made people really appreciate education and different cultures and, you know, and these people really took me in and it was nice. So we [the black and biracial students], it was a close-knit group, it was kind of like family within that high school.

She said about her college transition,

When I came here it was like, I'm gonna go to [college] and it's gonna kind of be the same as my high school. Cuz you know, here there's not many black people—it's on a larger scale, but it's the same kind of ratio. So I was asked to do a program [specifically for black students] the summer before freshman year, and naturally you're friends with thirty black people right away. So that was great and you know, finally it was like, oh, they don't care that I'm so light-skinned or whatever, so that was nice.

Kathy's experience is illustrative because it provides a critical case that defies the simplicity of using the number of black social networks for understanding how an individual may develop a border identity. In this case, Kathy underwent the greatest degree of rejection by her black peers when she was in an environment with a large number of African Americans. Attending a school where 50 percent of the students were black provided her with numerous opportunities to form friendships with other black students (as compared to a school with a lower black student population). In this environment, however, she reports feeling "rejected" by black women and avoiding interaction with black men. Here, her racial identity as biracial was not validated. Kathy's black peers considered her black, yet stigmatized her because of her physical appearance. This ran counter to her self-understanding as biracial. In this particular context, her declaration of a biracial identity was interpreted by her black peers as an anti-black sentiment. In their eyes, she is trying to establish herself as "better than," or "beyond" black. In her own eyes, she is attempting to provide an authentic expression of her racial identity. The result is conflict. In fact, the coupling of her appearance and her self-identification as biracial caused numerous interactional ruptures (such as gum being thrown in her "good hair" and several fist fights). From Kathy's perspective, the rejection she experienced by black women was counterbalanced by friendships with white peers who were similar in socioeconomic status and among whom her biracial identity was accepted. It was in the context of this simultaneous failure to be accepted as biracial by blacks and acceptance as biracial by whites that Kathy developed her understanding of biracialism as a border identity.

Once Kathy transferred to a predominately white school, however, with fewer blacks to "contend with," her closest network of friendships shifted from exclusively white to inclusive of black and biracial students. This environment was substantively different from her previous school with different "types" of students. The black students at her new school were affluent and, because they were in an environment where they were a visible minority, they had a strong vested interest in mutual self-acceptance. In this group, composed of blacks who accepted her as biracial and several other biracial peers, she found further validation for her particular self-identification and her understanding of biracialism as a border identity.

Finally, Kathy's transition to college further illustrates the importance of examining the type of social interaction an individual has within any given social network. Again, Kathy was in an environment in which blacks were a small and highly visible minority (less than 2 percent of the student body). Here, the pattern of her high school relationships was repeated, facilitated by ties made during the college summer program. She was accepted as biracial by a small, cohesive group of black students at a predominantly white institution while maintaining a core group of white friends. These experiences solidified her racial identity as exclusively biracial.

Specific sociodemographic factors may enable one individual to have access to differing types of social networks that would be unavailable to others. Social networks provide the terrain in which identities may be negotiated; in particular, nonexistent identities may emerge in the social setting, allowing participants to understand an individual's presence within a particular network. It is in these networks that the key process of interactional validation occurs and contributes to the differential choices of racial identity for biracial individuals.

Singular Identity

The singular identity differs from the option previously discussed because, as opposed to creating a new category of identification, an individual chooses between the two existing racial categories and identifies as exclusively one or the other. In the case of black/white biracials, the choices are either to identify exclusively as African American or exclusively as white. Because only a small number of our respondents identified as white, the singular black identity is the focus of this discussion.

Factors similar to those operating in the case of the border identity also influence people's choice of the singular black identity, although these factors work in different ways. Appearance, once again, plays an influential role in whether or not an individual will choose this particular identity strategy. Our data suggest that if an individual's appearance is close to what is typically taken to be black in the United States, he or she is more likely to identify as exclusively black, as opposed to biracial or white. In addition to appearance (which is more fully explored in Chapter 5), three socialization variables influence the choice of this identity option: social network composition, family discussion about being biracial, and experience of negative treatment from whites.

The racial composition of an individual's social network influences which racial identity options biracials choose. This relationship is strongest for those choosing the singular black and border identities. Those choosing the singular black identity are more likely than those choosing any other identity option to have come from black pre-adult social contexts. As adults, they continue to exist in social networks that are heavily populated with African Americans. Within these social networks, individuals have frequent interactions with blacks, which may increase the likelihood that they will come to understand their racial identity as African American, as opposed to any of the other identity options.

As previously suggested, racial identity choice is determined not only by the racial composition of social networks but also by how individuals experience race within a particular context. The second socialization factor of interest here is the experience of negative treatment (or lack thereof) by blacks and whites. There are both push and pull factors at work when an individual chooses a singular black identity. The push factors come from the experience of negative treatment by whites and the pull from the lack of such negative experiences by blacks. We know that the more other people treat an individual as part of a group, the more strongly that group becomes a part of the person's social identity. If a biracial person appears black, exists in a predominately black social network, is accepted as black—by blacks—and simultaneously experiences negative treatment by whites as an out-group member, it becomes easy to understand how that individual has developed, and actively maintains, a racial identity that is exclusively black.

When we broaden the conception of social network structure to move beyond racial composition and engage the social relations that occur within it, we must consider the effects of familial socialization on racial identity choice. Parental socialization as it occurs through verbal interactions within the family context was important for those choosing a singular black identity. Family discussion about being biracial may take on a variety of differing forms and dimensions. Individuals who did not talk openly in their family about being biracial and who did not experience negative treatment from blacks were the most likely to understand their racial identity as exclusively black. We asked respondents, "Did your family talk openly about being biracial?" Interview data suggest two different interpretations of a *no* response. The first is that the family simply did not discuss race as a salient element of everyday life, nor was the racial socialization of children in the family done in a conscious, verbalized manner. The second interpretation is that the family did not discuss being biracial as a legitimate identity option. Dee provided the following characterization of her family's "talk about being biracial":

They didn't sit me down and talk about like "you're biracial" and all that. My dad [black], whenever he would talk to us—he was the main one who talked to us about things—and he would say, "Well, being black, you're gonna have these problems in life and you're gonna have to know how to deal with them." So he never really addressed the fact that we were biracial, my dad was like "you're black."

When we compare the border and singular identities, it is clear that specific factors influence identity choice, albeit in different ways. Those who identify as black have a variety of others in their lives validating their blackness through direct means (discriminatory behavior by whites) and indirect means (a failure to discuss biracialism at home). They are pushed toward a black identity by their negative experiences with whites while being pulled toward a black identity by their acceptance from blacks. Their racial identity emerges, and is continually maintained, through the ongoing process of appearing to others as black, being categorized by others as black, and experiencing the world socially as a black person.

Protean Identity

The protean identity differs from the singular black and border identities because the individual does not possess a single, unified racial identity. Instead, the biracial person possesses multiple racial identities and personas that may be called up in appropriate contexts. Instead of identifying as biracial, black, or white consistently, the individual will sometimes identify as black, at other times as white, and still other times as biracial. The identity that is called up as representing the self is dependent solely on the individual's assessment of what is most appropriate or desirable in any given social setting. Unique to this identity strategy is the ability to be accepted as an in-group member by different groups, which requires a complex mastery of various cultural norms and values and an ongoing awareness and monitoring of the presentation of self.

Exploring a case from the interview data provides an illustration of the contextual shifting characteristic of this identity and an explanation as to why an individual may develop this understanding of what it means to be biracial. A respondent named Matt discussed how his dual cultural competencies allowed for him to function as an insider in differing social groups. Matt grew up in an all-white neighborhood and attended predominantly white private schools his entire life. His father, who was African American, was a prominent figure in the small town where he was raised. Despite their geographic distance, Matt did have frequent contact with his black extended family. He felt that his particular circumstances growing up helped him develop both middle-class white and black cultural competencies and simultaneous multiple identities. In the following excerpt from our conversation, he uses table manners to illustrate his perception of the subtleties of contextual shifting:

> Because of their [his parents'] status, I always learned, you know, start with the outside fork and work your way in, and this one is for dessert, you know. So I know, I know not to eat like this [puts his elbows on the table]. But then again, at the same time, [respondent shifts to black vernacular] when it comes picnic time or some other time and some ribs is on the table, I'm not afraid to get my hands dirty and dig on in and eat

with my hands and stuff like that. [Respondent shifts back to Standard English.] I mean, I guess my, the shift is when I'm not afraid to function in either world.

Although his depiction is both exaggerated and stereotypical, it reveals his understanding of biracialism as having the ability to shift his self-label between what he perceives as black and white cultural contexts. In addition, his experience enables us to see that, from his perspective, black and white social networks were always separate and distinct entities, each calling for different behavior and ways of being. This sense of separate worlds was not necessarily negated by his nuclear family, which he described as not discussing his biracialism. Understanding Matt's racially fragmented existence, combined with a lack of family discussion about his racial identity, helps us better appreciate how he developed a protean identity and the contexts in which that self-understanding was maintained.

Matt's experiences are representative of the protean cases in our data, in that the individuals choosing the protean identity differed from those choosing the previous two identity strategies in the composition of their racial networks. Interestingly, they can be described as having racially mixed pre-adult and adult social networks, enabling them to have significant exposure to both blacks and whites. Their experience of race is truly protean according to our data, which may explain their self-perceived ability to move fluidly across cultural borders.

We anticipated that the respondents choosing the protean identity option would report feeling close to both blacks and whites. We expected this because their entire racial identity strategy is dependent on contact with and acceptance from both of these groups. This was in fact supported by our data. The protean group felt the closest to blacks of any of the identity groups (including those who chose the singular black identity). They simultaneously felt the closest to whites compared to any of the other identity groups (including those who chose the singular white identity).

The protean case once again highlights the idea of identity-as-process. Individuals who chose this strategy of racial identity were influenced by the same factors as the border and singular identifiers; however, their response was not to integrate their racially fragmented experiences (like the border identifiers) nor to accept one reality and eschew another (like the singular identifiers). Instead, the protean respondents describe themselves as moving in and out of differing social contexts, acting as chameleons who change their identities as quickly and as often as others change their clothes. They are neither compromised nor ashamed of their "shifty" ways and find themselves validated at each and every turn.

Transcendent Identity

The final type of identity that biracial individuals choose is the nonracial or transcendent identity. This choice is different from the others because the individual consciously denies having any racial identity whatsoever. Individuals who choose this type of self-understanding simply do not use race as a construct to understand the social world or their relative place in it.

Not unlike the border, singular, and protean identities, appearance is the most salient factor influencing individuals to choose this particular racial identity. We originally assumed that having a white appearance, or the ability to "pass," would be crucial to the development of a transcendent self-understanding. It seemed to us that this identity option would be uniquely and exclusively available to individuals whose appearance had a high degree of ambiguity. We reasoned that if a biracial person's physical appearance was white, then he or she would not experience race socially in the same way as someone who physically looks African American. Because the logic of racial group categorization is based on the ability of others to immediately recognize a person's group membership, a white-appearing biracial person will consistently be assumed to be white and therefore experience the world as a white person. It is often easy for whites to assume a "color-blind" ideology because they do not experience the negativity of racial discrimination in their everyday lives and overlook the privileges of their whiteness. Given that, we assumed it would be equally easy for white-appearing biracial people to espouse a nonracial identity because they are treated, by default, as white. All the transcendent respondents in the Phase 1 interviews were white-appearing; therefore, we expected that this pattern would hold in the survey sample. In addition, we anticipated that they would be similar to the white ethnics described by Waters, who have the choice of whether or not to reveal their ethnicity in any given interaction.[41]

What we found in the survey sample was quite different from what we expected. In fact, respondents choosing the transcendent identity option included individuals along the full spectrum of physical appearance. They varied in both their self-reported skin color and their descriptions of how others perceive them. In other words, the transcendent respondents in Phase 2 were not exclusively white in appearance, as they were in the Phase 1 sample. Appearance did, however, influence their choice of racial identity. The relationship between appearance and the transcendent option is particularly complex, and for that reason, we discuss it thoroughly in Chapter 5.

When we consider the social network structure of respondents who choose the transcendent identity, it differs from those choosing the border, singular, and protean identity options. Transcendents had the whitest social networks of all respondents. In addition, they experienced the greatest amount of continuity between their pre-adult and adult social networks. Specifically, those who chose the transcendent identity option existed in white social contexts throughout their life span.

The transcendent respondents also differed from the rest of the sample in their feelings of closeness to blacks and whites. Reinforcing the characteristic aloofness of this identity option, they reported feeling equally close to whites and blacks. Their responses indicated that they did not feel particularly close to either blacks or whites, which was consistent with their position of not believing in the reality of racial identifiers. In fact, based on their stated feelings about the social construction of racial categories, we could picture the transcendent respondents rolling their eyes in disgust and annoyance while filling out the survey, as they did during the in-depth interviews.

The transcendent identity option proved to be more complex than we originally believed. Where we had once viewed the transcendent respondents as possessing a superficial color-blind mentality generated from a white appearance, youthful idealism, and/or a lack of experience with the harsh realities of racial stratification, we were forced to reconceptualize this option, given the intricacies of the data. Our analysis of the determinants of a transcendent identity, as opposed to any of the other available options, led us to view the transcendents as truly on the fringe of race-as-reality. Their perspective was not the typical color-blind ideology because, although they wished less attention were paid to race, they were acutely aware of how race negatively affects the daily existence of people of color. In contrast to our initial assumptions, they were not immune to negative experiences, nor were they all physically white in appearance. They had experienced discrimination, yet they responded by intellectualizing those situations as part of a broad societal problem; one in which they were deeply embedded. This authentic stranger's perspective was not difficult for them because they failed to have a racial identity that would necessitate an emotional response. This lack of a racialized self-understanding meant there simply were no feelings to be hurt, no adjustments to be made, and no racial identity to validate or contest in daily social interaction.

Discussion

Our goal in this chapter was to explain why biracial people make differing choices about their racial identities; we used the existing literature on the determinants of both white ethnic identity and black identity. Although we found that appearance, social network composition, and socialization factors explained the various choices biracial people make, those factors work differently in each of the four racial identity models presented in this chapter. This, we believe, reinforces our conceptualization of biracial identity as a multidimensional phenomenon. Being biracial means different things to different segments of the mixed-race population, and people construct different ideas about their racial identity based on varying sets of social experiences.

The models set forth in this chapter also support the idea of blending what we know about white ethnic options and the factors that determine racial identity within the African American population to create a framework that explains racial identity choice among biracial people. Several factors that have consistently predicted black racial identity (age, geographic location, religious participation) and white ethnic identity (surname, knowledge about an ethnicity, group popularity) failed to aid in explaining biracial identity in our analysis of interview data. However, appearance, social network composition, and family and peer socialization factors were salient in explaining identity choice in our interview data. Therefore, we included them in the Survey of Biracial Experiences. Our analysis of the survey data illustrated the power of that new framework. Because it required ideas from both of these bodies or research, we believe that biracial identity, and therefore its determinants, can be considered methodologically and conceptually unique from both black identity and white ethnic identity.

Finally, the findings presented in this chapter support our reliance on interactional validation as the key mechanism underlying identity construction and maintenance. It is the validation process that unifies the respondents. What differentiates them is from whom and for what they seek validation. Respondents choosing each of the four strategies are looking for different identities to be validated by different groups of people, yet their racial identity involves the interactional process of presenting an identity, having that identity recognized by others, and experiencing either validation or rejection. The following chapter examines the critical effect of appearance in this process.

5

The Color Complex

Appearance and Biracial Identity

The connections among skin color (phenotype), race (racial classification), and racial identity (racial self-understanding) appear straightforward. If your phenotype is dark or "black," then you are categorized as black and you should think of yourself as black. On the other hand, if your phenotype is light or "white," then you are classified as such and understand yourself as white. Indeed, for most individuals, this correlation is infallible, deterministic, and reliable. A moment's thought provides clear evidence that this assumed, closely linked trinity of color-race-identity (a relationship legally and culturally codified through the one-drop rule) is fallible, is *not* deterministic, and is unreliable and unstable as it changes over time. Available arguments and evidence suggest that this triumvirate is much more complicated at the turn of the century.[1] In addition, we have come to acknowledge that the assumption has existed only to serve the powers that be—powers that have been typically associated with white desires to divide and conquer people of color.[2] If, in fact, society continues to set tight parameters of identity options for mixed-race individuals by assuming the relationship between color, race, and identity, then the racialized social structure will continue unchanged. Biracial individuals and the idea of biracialism represent a challenge to that scenario.

The truth of the matter is that skin colors exist in a wide array—a spectrum from the darkest phenotype to the lightest. Although it may be true that most people would place those who have dark skin into the black race and those with light skin into the white race, this alone is not proof of a correlation between phenotype and race. This assumption becomes even more problematic when there is a presumption that racial identity is also correlated with this relationship. Darker-skinned individuals may not racially identify themselves as black, and lighter-skinned individuals may not racially identify themselves as white. We know that the categories of black and white are social constructions—imperfect indicators of both racial categorization and, more important for our purposes, racial identity.[3] Thus, race (as a concept) is constructed and fundamentally fallible, racial categorization is full of pitfalls, and racial identity is a phenomenon as nebulous as the previous two. To apply the social and cultural correlation of skin color to these processes is much more complicated than commonly assumed. This complexity grows deeper when we consider that biracial individuals' skin colors truly encompass the spectrum of possible phenotypes. Those holding the previously stated assumptions would predict that biracial individuals whose skin is darker would tend to choose the singularly black identity and align themselves most closely with the black community. Analogously, those who have light skin would be more likely to choose a border identity or possibly a singular white self-understanding, aligning themselves more closely with the white community. These represent social and cultural push and pull factors that may affect the racial self-understanding of biracial individuals. However, stated this way, they present a simplistic assumption of race held by many in the United States, an assumption with serious implications for individuals' lives and opportunities. These presumptions and the relationships predicated on them are explored in this chapter.

Focusing on the biracial experience enables a fertile exploration of how culture influences identity or how socially constructed, cognitive understandings of differing racial categories interact with significant symbols to influence the way in which people understand themselves and their relationship to others. The most salient symbol representing group membership is a person's appearance. It is important to focus on appearance for several reasons. First and foremost, the discussion in previous chapters indicated the importance of physical appearance in understanding the different choices that biracial individuals make about their identity and why they make those choices. Even more interesting, appearance plays a different and at times counterintuitive role in each of the various identity options. Theoretically, appearance is fundamentally important to the process of human interaction because people are unable to observe directly the intentions and character of individuals.[4] It is through appearance that people evaluate themselves as well as others and through which people present themselves to others.[5] It is also the terrain in which the discourse of race is fueled. Appearance presents our identity to others in social interaction. At the same time, it allows us to infer others' identities, help define the situation, and provide a cognitive context for the actors involved. In this sense, appearance can become a reality in and of itself.[6]

Using the typology of the racial identities described in previous chapters, we explore the appearance-identity link among our biracial respondents. To this end, we briefly discuss the historical background of the color-race-identity triad and its historical connection with systems of social stratification in various contexts. This discussion includes a review the literature on the relationship between phenotype and racial identity for biracial individuals. Unlike the case with ethnic options, appearance plays a counterintuitive role in the way biracial people choose their racial identity. Through investigating the appearance-identity link with an emerging demographic group, we can grasp the power of cultural influences and social interaction over the process of constructing and understanding racial identities. Gregory Stone's work on appearance serves as the theoretical underpinning for our use of appearance as the building block for a larger interpretive model to understand biracial identity. We briefly restate Stone's thesis on the relationships between appearance and identity, expand the model to encompass master statuses or universal identities, and explore the interpretive power of the model by examining data from case studies and the Survey of Biracial Experiences (see Appendix F). The purpose of this expansion and discussion is to grasp the power of cultural influences and social interaction in the process of identity construction and maintenance.

Research on Phenotype and Racial Identity

The empirical literature on the effects of skin color, the most salient of all bodily appearance characteristics for discussions of race, further illuminates the importance of appearance. Skin color has been found to affect mate and friend selection, a variety of life chances and opportunities, and mental illness.[7] Verna Keith and Cedric Herring have shown that skin color remains one of the present-day mechanisms influencing resource distribution in America.[8] The phenotype literature, however, has not addressed the issues of how individuals of color perceive their own racial identity nor of how phenotype might play a role in the racial self-understandings of people of color. The appearance of biracial individuals is often ambiguous, and these individuals exist in a variety of social contexts of differing racial composition. According to the commonsense assumption that race is a biological as opposed to a socially constructed reality, individuals' physical traits determine racial group membership. Therefore, an individual's phenotype should determine racial identity. The caveat to this system is the one-drop rule, which mandates that above and beyond phenotypic categorizations, anyone with a black ancestor is black (regardless of appearance). Exploring the influence of appearance on identity for biracials allows us to join and extend the literature by understanding how our presentations of self and the reviews of others are reflexive and function within a socially constructed set of parameters.

Early research, built on the assumption of the one-drop rule, was inadequate in identifying the complexities of racial identity among biracials in the United States. This being the case, the relationship between phenotype and racial identity remained unquestioned and was rarely the focus of empirical investigation. Methodological problems in collecting data on biracial individuals, coupled with samples revealing little variation in phenotypes, made exploration of the relationship between phenotype and racial identity among biracials difficult. The lack of empirical study is associated with the paucity of theoretical development of the appearance-identity link. The research on biracials in the 1970s and early 1980s never investigated the role of appearance in identity formation because people assumed that regardless of your physical appearance, if you had a black parent then you were black.

Several researchers have given the appearance-identity question passing comments that transcend the one-drop assumption.[9] Philip Brown's research demonstrates that appearance is an important factor in the emotional and cognitive attitude individuals have toward themselves, and he discusses the importance of physical appearance for biracials.[10] He implies that the darker-skinned the biracial individuals, the more likely they would be to adopt and develop an exclusively black identity. However, he also theorizes that factors such as the ratio of blacks to whites in given socialization contexts could influence this relationship; he does not specify how. Similarly, G. Reginald Daniel has discussed how the intricate interrelationships between socialization experiences and the broader social and cultural context of race relations can influence the appearance-identity link; however, he provided no clear hypotheses.[11] Dorcas Bowles, describing the treatment of biracial clients with the goal of developing a healthy biracial identity, found that women had a more difficult time accepting their black physical features than men; thus, a possible gender interaction with phenotype was indicated in the influence on identity.[12] Barbara Tizard and Ann Phoenix found that white-appearing biracials were unlikely to identify exclusively as black.[13] Although several scholars believe that physical appearance is crucial to the development and maintenance of a racial identity among biracials, the research has not rigorously investigated the appearance-identity link. This is not surprising, given that the scarcity of theoretical work provides little guidance for empirical investigation.

The research on biracial identity has often cited the reactions of whites to biracial individuals. It was Kathy Russell, Midge Wilson, and Ronald Hall's *The Color Complex* that really tackled the issue of the politics of skin color among African Americans, albeit on a popular as opposed to scholarly level.[14] Certainly, the one-drop rule, created and so closely monitored by whites, served to set parameters on the identity options of biracial individuals; *The Color Complex* explored the black community's role in maintaining color preferences.

Russell and her colleagues considered the black community's love/hate relationship with the one-drop rule and with skin color. They argued that because of historical preferences grounded in slavery, light-skinned blacks and mulattos have disproportionately gained financial advantages. This preferential treatment of mulattos by whites served as the foundation for a social and cultural system of color classism within black America. Generational advantages secured by those of lighter skin were evident, and mulattos, in an attempt to preserve their status, segregated themselves into communities and discriminated against darker members of the larger black community.

The Color Complex provides evidence that those members of the community with the lightest skin and the most Caucasian-looking features have been allowed the greatest freedoms and have achieved at higher rates. The authors go further to display the ways in which darker-skinned members of the black community discriminate against mixed-race individuals in the workplace, how patterns of dating within the community are tangled up with phenotype, how networks are constructed or dismantled on the basis of color classism, and how blacks use unique cultural coding (tertiary clues such as hair, first names, etc.) to distinguish between those who are black and those who are not. Yet the authors do not shy away from the other side of the coin in their argument: biracial individuals have benefited from their lighter skin and have, in many ways, cultivated a sense of elitism within the black community. Although Russell and her colleagues expose color distinctions and dissension among African Americans, they do not discuss the relationship between color and identity.

Currently, researchers have done little more than speculate about the relationship between appearance and racial identity among biracial individuals. Although there has been little or no theoretical development on this relationship, one important addition has been to broaden the conceptualization of appearance. We consider color to be both a personal and a social characteristic; that is, people perceive their skin color, but they also interpret their appearance through the eyes of others within any given interactional sphere.[15] Both Maria Root and Kerry Ann Rockquemore highlight the inherent problem that exists when there is a mismatch between appearance and identity.[16] In other words, it would be extremely difficult for a person to choose an exclusively black or exclusively white identity if his or her physical appearance did not match the chosen identity. Although this may seem obvious, the reality of the racial identity choices that biracial individuals make is much more than skin deep.

The Situated Self: Stone and Appearance

Stone has described identity as establishing what and where an actor is in social terms.[17] It is not a substitute word for *self* but, instead, describes the self as situated. The self is cast in the shape of a social object by the acknowledgment of the actor's participation or membership in social relations. The presenter's identity is validated when others in an interactional context are able to place the actor as a social object by assigning to that person the same words of identity that the actor uses in self-description. When an individual's asserted placement is acknowledged by others, that identity becomes a public meaning of the self, despite the fact that the public meaning may or may not coincide with the presenter's intended meaning. This dialectical process of potential mutual agreement, Stone argues, is stimulated by symbols of appearance.[18] Mutual identification is an ongoing dance of reflexive social processes. Stone refers to these processes as *apposition* and *opposition,* a simultaneous bringing together and setting apart. People are able to locate and understand others in particular situations (as social objects) by bringing them together with other social objects so that they are similarly situated. At the same time that people engage in this bringing together, they differentiate or set the actor apart from other social objects. For Stone, "identity is intrinsically associated with all the joinings and departures of social life."[19] For an identity to be publicly and personally meaningful, an individual must be concurrently joined with some social objects while separated from others by both the self and others.

Situating the other is only one aspect of the mutual identification process. Situating is followed by an additional simultaneous set of processes: identification *of* and identification *with.* These two processes are interdependent in that people cannot identify with another without having identified, or placed, the other. Role taking is one form of identifying with, as is sympathy. Mutual identification is typically facilitated by appearance and initiated without verbal communication. Stone gives the example of gender in that people do not verbally inquire about others' status as male or female, yet a person's sex category must be established because it structures the parameters of any given interaction. People come to know the other's sex category because it is silently established through appearance.[20] It becomes clear at this point that appearance establishes an actor's basic universal identification; hence, appearance functions as a form of communication that is very different from discourse. Stone argues that appearance "sets the stage for, permits, sustains, and delimits the possibilities of discourse by underwriting the possibilities for meaningful discussion."[21]

Stone conceptually defines identity as an ongoing process of mutual identification. He frames social interaction as the context of identity establishment, arguing that it is necessary to break down a social transaction into its communicative parts. Communication, he argues, can be divided into two equally relevant parts: (a) discourse and (b) appearance. Discourse refers to the substance of what is being verbally communicated between actors, whereas appearance serves as a nonverbal source of communication.

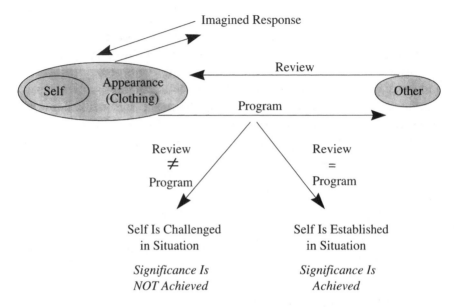

Figure 5.1. Stone's Appearance Model Within an Interactional Situation

Appearance not only communicates identity but also has a reflexive relationship with identity. Appearance simultaneously presents a person's identity and serves as the source of identity (or as a mask to hide identities). Despite establishing that a reflexive relationship exists, Stone's work does not expand on the latter function of appearance. Instead, he focuses on how appearance functions as a situator in the process of face-to-face interaction. Through appearance, the self presents an identity. Because Stone uses empirical data to explore his theoretical model, he must limit the use of appearance to a singular observable dimension. He chooses to focus on clothing as an operationalization of the theoretical concept of appearance. To justify this selection, Stone argues that a person's clothes impart value to the wearer both in the wearer's own eyes and in the eyes of others.[22] In response to his or her clothes, the wearer is cast as a social object or given some identity. If the self (as object) is established by appearance, then the meaning of appearance can be studied by examining the responses mobilized by an actor's clothing. Figure 5.1 is a schematic representation of our interpretation of Stone's theoretical framework. The influence of George Herbert Mead's seminal work in this area is clear as he searches for the meaning of appearance in the responses that it mobilizes.[23] Hence, Stone relies on a fundamentally interactionist understanding and focuses his work on the responses to an individual's appearance within the context of social interaction. The model specifies three separate responses: (a) the program, (b) the review, and (c) the self's imagined response of the other.[24] Stone uses the term *program* to describe the responses made about individual actors by the actors themselves. The second set of responses, the *reviews*, are made about the actors by others with whom they interact. There is an additional third type of response which Stone specifies is relevant but which is outside the limits of his empirical investigation. This third type of response is the actors' imagination of others' responses to their appearance and resultant initial self-feeling.[25]

Programs and reviews agree with each other when the self has presented an identity and that identity is accepted by the other within the process of social interaction. When this agreement occurs, the self of the person who appears, or the actor whose appearance has elicited the desired response, is validated. Disagreement occurs when the program and the response do not agree. In this case, the self of the actor who appears is challenged. Behavior between the actors may be directed toward a redefinition or renegotiation of the challenged self. Challenges and validations of the self, according to Stone, are initially aroused by self and others' response to an actor's personal appearance.

Drawing on the work of Mead and Charles Horton Cooley, Stone argues that the self's responses to one's appearance are reflexive in character.[26] His idea of mutual identification implies that when people place others, they engage in a complementary placing of themselves so that each actor's "place" is relative to the "place of others." When people respond to others' appearance, they respond to their own appearance as well. Reviews and programs are intricately linked because people's programs parallel their reviews of others. Stone believes that "one appears, reflects upon that appearance, and appropriates words of identity and attitude for himself in response to that appearance."[27] By appearing, people announce their identity. If the meaning of the appearance is "supplied" by the reviews others make of their appearance, it is established or consensually validated by the relative coincidence of such reviews with the program of the person who appears. In other words, if an actor's clothing calls out in others the same identifications of the wearer as it calls out in the wearer, the appearance is situationally meaningful. By way of appearance, then, selves are established and mobilized. From this theoretical model, Stone defines the self as "any validated program which exercises a regulatory function over other responses of the same organism, including the formulation of other programs."[28] The meaning of appearance, therefore, is the establishment of identity for the actors who appear by the coincident programs and reviews awakened by their appearance.

Expanding the Appearance-Identity Model

Stone has asserted that there are multiple types of identities, the varieties of which are isomorphic with the varieties of social relations. He suggests early on that there are at least four different types used to place and announce the identities communicated by appearance: (a) universal words designating a person's humanity (such as age and gender), (b) names and nicknames, (c) titles, and (d) relational categories. Left out of the discussion of universal identities is race. Therefore, the first way we must extend Stone's model is by joining the idea of appearance as the source of identity and the reality of the cultural context in which the actor operates. In American society, certain physical characteristics signify racial group membership. Because this signifier also carries with it a historical tradition of stratification and stigmatization, we recognize this particular appearance as a master status.[29] Race, as a master status, is a singular identity that has the power to subsume most other role-related identities. For example, a person is not simply a student but, rather, a "black student" or a "student of color."

When working with an identity that is a master status, it becomes necessary to reexamine the reflexive capacity of the appearance-identity link. We have explored Stone's analysis of how appearance presents identity, but appearance is also the source of identity because others respond to people in terms of their appearance and body-derived identities that are both constructed and imposed in the situation. To use Stone's appearance model in understanding racial identity, we must expand his conceptual framework to encompass these particularities.

A person's physical body is, in social psychological terms, a collection of cultural meanings that supply basic information and interpretations to others. Race refers not to a genetically based reality but to the symbolic

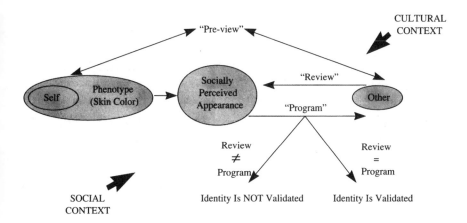

Figure 5.2. The Influence of Appearance on Biracial Identity

meaning of bodily differences. For this reason, bodily characteristics, specifically skin color, facial features, and hair texture, define the actor in a way that forces language to become a secondary appearance cue; clothing is relegated to a tertiary status. Because American cultural coding imposes a uniquely dichotomous black/non-black schema of racial identification, race functions as a socially general or universal interactional resource. We must reiterate that race, as a universal category of identity, is subtly important to most social interactions because of its link to the distribution of power and status in society. Physical characteristics are inescapable signifiers used as the context for designation of an actor's social group membership. These signifiers provide individuals with an immediate basis for identification of the other and set up the parameters in which the universe of discourse takes place.

The second fundamental way in which we would like to expand Stone's model is by addressing his limited conception of the self. Stone depicts a truncated version of the self, one that represents an objectively biased cognitive reduction of the self as process. Specifically, Stone's self focuses on the *self* as object without considering the subjective element or the *self as subject*. Stone's version of identity provides a window to the self as situated, but he has limited himself in being able to deal with how the situated self knows itself, not as social object but as subject. Andrew Weigert makes this critique and posits an alternative formulation of the self, the *substantival self*. He defines self as "an actor 1. Whose action is conceptualized as intending behavior; 2. Whose consciousness of such behavior is characterized by concomitant awareness of the self in action; and 3. Who thus possesses the capacity of being both subject and object to himself."[30] This conception of self allows us to think more expansively about the relationship between the self and identity and allows for a deeper contextualization of the function of appearance.

We add that within Stone's model we also draw out the subjective elements of the self by capitalizing on his idea of the "imagined response of the other." He suggests that the self in action has the capacity to view and interpret the responses of the other. Can we not also consider that the actor, in addition to this, has the capacity to anticipate the other's review, know that it is reflecting on that review, and consciously use that imagined response to formulate a program? In other words, we are suggesting that the actor may consciously assess the other to gauge and estimate the review (we can say the actor is making a "pre-view") and use that estimation to calculate and manipulate the program put forth or the identity presented.[31] It will become easier to assess the usefulness of the "preview" later in the discussion of the case studies and survey results. Figure 5.2 is a schematic representation of our extension of Stone's conceptual framework. Although we have suggested several limitations of the model for interpreting racial identity, we have retained Stone's fundamental processes of situating the other as social object and mutual identification. Appearance provides the parameters for social interaction and may have the capacity to validate or challenge the self that is presented. In the following sections, we examine data from both the in-depth interviews and the Survey of Biracial Experiences to assess whether or not appearance represents the terrain in which embodied selves are established and mobilized, as suggested in the previous discussion. The extended theoretical model provides a sense of the processes of identity construction and maintenance with respect to racial identities. Survey data and in-depth case studies of biracial individuals who have diverse bodily characteristics, varying appearance, and different understandings of their selves as biracial allow us to see how their racial identities emerge through the process of mutual (mis)identification.

The above discussion reveals several propositions concerning the link between appearance and the racial identity choices of biracial individuals. We measure physical appearance in two ways: (a) self-reported skin color and (b) respondents' perceptions of how others racially categorize them. We discuss these two distinct variables as *skin color* and *appearance*, respectively. Concerning the first personal appearance characteristic, skin color, we expected that *skin color will not directly affect racial identity*. We anticipated this to be the case because the pre-view made by biracial individuals about their own appearance is based on both the imagined response of others in interactions and on others' reviews of the biracial individuals' presentation of self.

Regarding the second social appearance characteristic, appearance, which is created by the biracial individuals' understanding of their skin color as well as the pre-view and review (which are both rooted in the judgments of others in interactions), we expected that it was appearance, not skin color, that influenced the racial identification of biracials and that skin color was a part of and worked through a person's appearance to affect identity. Therefore, our second proposition was that *an actor's socially perceived appearance will affect racial identity even after controlling for skin color.*

Finally, we investigated key social factors—the racial composition of pre-adult social contexts and negative treatment by whites and/or blacks—to assess how social context may alter the appearance-identity link. We are particularly interested in examining the effects of racial differences in social network composition on the appearance-identity link because it is within these social contexts that the interactional parameters for identity are established. Therefore, our final proposition was that the *racial composition of social contexts will moderate the effect of appearance on racial identity.*

Sample Variation in Appearance

Chapter 2 described the sample of biracial individuals obtained for use in this study and the fact that it varies on many dimensions of interest. For an investigation of the appearance-identity link, this sample contains variation in several important areas: phenotype, appearance, racial identity, and contextual experiences of race. Before discussing the results, it is important to indicate the diversity in the sample on these key variables.

Within our sample, there exists wide variation in self-reported skin color. We asked respondents to describe their skin color along a predefined skin color gradient ranging from 0 = *white* to 12 = *black*.[32] The median score is 6, but the variation is striking. We also will consider results from analysis using the original skin color variable collapsed into roughly three equal categories: light (0-3), medium (4-8), and dark (9-12) skin. Within the sample, about 34 percent of respondents reported their skin as light, 39 percent as medium, and 25 percent percent as dark. Respondents, by their own estimation, assessed their skin color as ranging across the phenotypic spectrum. This variance is critical to our analysis because it allows us to explore the influence of skin color on the choices that our respondents make about their racial identity.

In addition, respondents differ in their answers to the question about their socially mediated appearance. Once again, variation in responses does exist; however, the majority of respondents (56.2 percent) described their appearance as "ambiguous though most people assume I am black" (although they had reported wide variation in skin color). About 17 percent stated that they "appear black, most people assume I am black," whereas another 16 percent stated that they were "ambiguous, most people do not assume I am black." Finally, 10 percent of our sample of biracials said they "appear white, I could 'pass' as white." These descriptive measures reveal two facts that are crucial to our forthcoming discussion: (a) the sample includes variation on the two key measures of appearance set forth in our theoretical model and (b) the differences between these two variables suggests that they are, in fact, indicating two conceptually distinct elements of appearance.

There is also significant variation in the contextual experience of race of these respondents. These biracials came from a variety of pre-adult socialization contexts with varying racial compositions. For the discussion in this chapter, the original variable was collapsed into one with roughly equal proportions: predominantly white contexts (32.8 percent), mixed black/white contexts (33.3 percent), and predominantly black contexts (33.9 percent).[33] Besides differences in pre-adult socialization experiences, our respondents varied in the ways they experienced race socially. Most of them reported experiencing negative treatment from blacks (60.5 percent), and even more of them reported experiencing negative treatment from whites (74.3 percent).[34]

The Relationship Between Phenotype, Appearance, and Racial Identity Among Biracial Individuals

One way our expansion of Stone's model allows us to clarify unresolved issues in the literature concerning color and identity is that appearance is both multifaceted *and* reflexive. Our expanded model of the appearance-identity link led us to make the distinction between self-perceived *skin color* and socially mediated *appearance*. Our data analysis reveals that within the four types of socially mediated appearance there exists significant variation in self-perceived skin color. For example, biracial individuals who say that they "appear white, and could pass" have self-perceived skin colors that vary from the lightest end to the middle range of the skin color gradient. Those who are "ambiguous" but who are "assumed to be black by others" have skin tones that encompass the entire spectrum of skin colors. Indeed, those who "appear white, and could pass" do, on average, perceive their skin color as lighter than the other types; however, there is significant variation in the perceived phenotypes of this group. Conversely, those who understand other people's reviews as stating that they "appear black" and therefore are assumed to be black perceive their own skin color as darker, on average, than the other types; yet, again, there is significant variation in these biracial individuals' skin colors as well.

We find that there is a very strong association between skin color and the way these individuals understand their appearance and vice versa. Among those who make pre-views that they "appear white and could pass," 64.7 percent perceive themselves as having light skin. Furthermore, the percentage of respondents with light skin continuously decreases as the pre-views these biracial individuals make become increasingly imbued with others' assumptions that they are black. Most (82.2 percent) of those who appear ambiguous and are not assumed to be black describe themselves as having light to medium skin. Of those who say they "appear black" and are assumed to be black by others, most (65.5 percent) perceive their skin color as dark. Interestingly, although skin color is associated with appearance, this association is not perfect. In other words, our respondent's self-reported skin color does not completely determine their pre-views or how they perceive the reviews of others. Nor do their pre-views of others' interpretations of their appearance wholly determine their self-perceived skin color. Perhaps, it is the context within which these interpretations take place that dictates just how strong a correlation there is between others' perceptions and an individual's self-perceptions. We consider this possibility later in this chapter.

Because mixed-race individuals' pre-views of their appearance are rooted in others' reviews of their appearance, we did not expect skin color to affect racial identity choices among biracial Americans. People may think they look black, but this thought is not created in isolation. The thought is constructed through interactions with others. If others think individuals look black, then those individuals may be categorized as such and may possibly think of themselves as black. However, an individual's self-perception of skin color alone would not be enough to push or pull a biracial individual's racial identity in one direction or another. Given the wide variety of skin tones present among biracial people, it seems clear that others play a large role in the racial identity choices these individuals make. Root has argued that, given the wide variations in skin tones within multiracial populations, skin color should not be expected to affect the racial self-identifications of biracial and multiracial people.[35] In addition, Russell and her colleagues suggested that, although color has been used as a metaphor for blackness, pigmentation alone cannot be used to predict the extent of racial identification and that "some of the most Afrocentric people in America are those with the least amount of African ancestry."[36]

In our data, there is no association between perceived skin color and the way that biracial individuals racially understand themselves. This provides supportive evidence for our first assertion. Clearly, the trinity of color-race-identity is detrimental. Here we have a population with widely varying skin tones, people who would be categorized as black yet may not understand themselves as black.

Our theoretical model (see Figure 5.2) led us to assert that because self-understanding is a process of the interaction between individuals and others *in context*, even the seemingly most personal element of the self, how people understand their own appearance, is fundamentally social.

Therefore, we expected biracial people's socially mediated appearance to influence racial identity rather than their skin color. In fact, appearance and racial identification among black/white biracials are strongly associated in this sample. The results can be most clearly understood by examining each of the various identity types and their unique link with appearance.

Unlike skin color, our measure of appearance operationalizes both the reviews of others and the racial assumptions others make about biracial individuals within social interactions. It is clear that these reviews and assumptions deeply affect biracials' self-understandings of their own race. The interview data provide unique insight into the mechanisms behind the strong association between socially mediated appearance and racial identity among this population. We now turn to an in-depth look at each of the identity types and how appearance plays a role in the development, maintenance, and renegotiation of each.

How Does Appearance Influence the Development of Differential Understandings of Biracial Identity?

In Chapter 3, we demonstrated that although we may categorize all individuals who have one black and one white biological parent as biracial, these people understand their racial identity in varying ways and may use different racial identifiers to describe themselves. We explore each of these different understandings to assess the interpretive power of the expanded conceptual model, primarily using data from the interviews and supplementing those findings with survey data.

It is clear from the survey data that the reviews of others significantly affect the racial identity choices of biracial individuals. Although the survey data illustrate descriptive patterns in the data, the qualitative data from the in-depth interviews provide richer insight into the mechanisms behind these patterns. Because the survey data and the in-depth interview data tap different aspects of the processes involved in the racial identification of biracial individuals, it is necessary to discuss the results in a specific manner. This method of discussing the findings provides insight into these complex relationships while offering researchers and students of racial identity potential avenues for future research to clarify the issues.[37]

Appearance and the Border Identity

As described in Chapter 3, some individuals with one black and one white parent understand being biracial as a border identity—a self that is de facto between existing social categories yet has a uniqueness all its own. It must be recognized immediately that this type of identification has only recently become available to individuals and still exists only in selected contexts within American society. Historically and traditionally (with the notable exception of specific and isolated instances discussed in Chapter 1), children of interracial marriages have typically been limited to a black racial identity (regardless of physical appearance) in accordance with the one-drop rule. Because biracial individuals have historically been considered members of the black community (regardless of their appearance), any racial identity other than black is a relatively new phenomenon. How then have these individuals developed and maintained a previously unacceptable and/or unavailable identity?

A common set of experiences existed among interview respondents who understood being biracial as a border identity. Many of the individuals were middle to uppermiddle class, educated in private schools, raised in predominately white neighborhoods, and had predominantly white friends and relatives in their social networks. In many of these cases, respondents were the only non-white person (or one of a few) in their schools and communities. Many were popular and active in sports and school activities or held leadership positions in their educational institutions. It is within this particular type of social context, combined with a homogeneous set of social networks, that these individuals were able to develop a self-understanding of being biracial as a border identity, an understanding that was not historically available (or at the very least was not validated by others).

It also became clear, in talking with these individuals, that they approximated their white peers in every way: in their language usage, tastes, mannerisms, and style. In fact, the only difference between them and their peers was the racial group membership of one of their parents (who may or may not have played a role in their upbringing) and their physical appearance. In the minds of their peers, respondents were more like them than they were different and did not fit into their cognitive conception of "black." Given that both the biracial individuals and the peers had little contact with blacks, their perceptions were largely stereotypical and media-derived. The result of this particular set of circumstances is that individuals repeatedly were told by their peers (in a complimentary fashion), "Well, I don't really think of you as black." This statement implies the following: (a) the speaker has a cognitive perception of what "black" is, (b) "black" is something different from what the speaker is (white), and (c) the biracial person does not fit into that category because he or she is more like the speaker (in the speaker's mind) than that person's understanding of "black." The result of this coincidental failure of mutual identification is for both parties to agree on a new category of identification, being biracial, where biracial means for both something between white and black. The survey data support this pattern among respondents choosing the validated border identity.

In our understanding of biracial identity, the border identity comprises two unique self-understandings constructed and maintained on the basis of interactions with others. If individuals possess a validated border identity, they understand themselves as uniquely biracial and their program is validated by others within their interactional sphere. This validation allows biracial people to maintain their racial self-understanding and make little or no alterations to their program. Unvalidated border individuals also consider themselves to be uniquely biracial; however, their program is not validated. Others primarily assume they are black, and therefore, they report experiencing the world as a black person, although they understand themselves as a biracial person. When people's racial program is not validated by others in their significant social network, they either alter their program or remain in a nebulous, marginal, and unresolved state with regard to their racial identity. The question we explore in this section is what difference does appearance make, if any, in the development and maintenance of a border identity? Specifically, are there differences, rooted in appearance, that distinguish between those biracial individuals whose border identity is validated versus those whose border identity is not?

When we look at the distribution of skin tones among both types of border identifiers, we find that both groups have a wide range of skin colors, averaging around the middle of the entire distribution. Although more respondents have an unvalidated border identity than a validated border identity, both groups are similar with regard to their self-perceived skin color. They see themselves as literally "in between" on the spectrum of possible phenotypes, and this perception does not influence whether or not others validate their unique self-understanding as biracial. What does seem to influence their validation, not surprisingly, is how they perceive others' perception of their appearance (i.e., their socially mediated appearance).

More than 60 percent of the biracials whose border identity is validated, and 62.5 percent of those whose identity is not validated, describe their appearance as "ambiguous but people assume I am black." However, this is stronger for those choosing the unvalidated border identity because they are more likely to be assumed black than those whose border identity is validated by others. In other words, 34.2 percent of those choosing the validated border identity are not perceived by others to be black, compared to only 15.6 percent of respondents in the unvalidated group. The reviews by others in the interactional spheres within which these biracials exist put salient parameters on their racial self-understandings. To desire a unique racial identity as a biracial person, and yet have others assume you are black, leads a biracial individual to become unable to maintain a border identity.

When we consider the process of mutual identification, interaction becomes difficult if individuals cannot be immediately and unconsciously placed into a particular category. Categorization is problematic when (a) bodily features are ambiguous, (b) the other has knowledge about the individual that complicates categorization (such as knowing that a person has one black and one white parent), or (c) the individual's secondary and tertiary cues (language and dress) do not fit into the other's preconceived ideas about members of a particular category. Any one or a combination of these factors can introduce difficulty into the mutual identification process. This difficulty is typically broken by addressing the identification problem directly. For example, biracial individuals often report being asked, "What are you?" to clarify an unclear program.[38] This question and answer series typically results in the introduction of a new category of meaning (biracial) where the two individuals renegotiate both the program and the review.

From this context of negotiated identification, we can begin to understand how a biracial individual could develop a self-understanding of biracial as a border identity regardless of bodily appearance. This category includes individuals who may be characterized from appearance alone as black. However, their white parentage, socialization in white middle-class networks, and the program they put forth may allow them to understand themselves as biracial and to be validated in their understanding as a border identity. This category also encompasses individuals whose physical characteristics are ambiguous (but not white) who have similar socialization experiences. Finally, this category includes those individuals who are "light enough to pass," or who look white, and who also share similar social experiences. In sum, regardless of the individuals' bodily characteristics, their understanding of their racial identity as being neither black nor white derives from the complexity of the mutual identification process and the ability of individual actors to negotiate a meaningful identity with a selected subset of white others.

The situation is entirely different for those border individuals whose identity is not renegotiated, where the process of mutual identification is seemingly bypassed and they are assumed to be black by others—the unvalidated border group. These individuals are trapped between the one-drop rule and the multiracial movement, both of which have worked to set parameters on the racial identities of biracial individuals. We fully explore this point in Chapter 6, where we examine the complex relationship between identity politics, the "reality" of racial categorization, and racial identity options.

Appearance and the Singular Identity

In addition to the border identity, there are individuals with one black and one white parent who understand being biracial as a singular identity. In this case, their racial identity is exclusively African American or exclusively white. For people having this understanding of their biracialism, it is a mere acknowledgment of the racial categorization of one of their birth parents. This is because the individual's cognitive conception of what it means to be black (or less commonly, white) is inclusive of a wide range of individual appearance and parental combinations. At the extreme, individuals acknowledge the existence of their (white or black) parent, but this is not salient in defining their self-understanding and may not be offered as identifying information unless specifically requested.

In Chapter 3, we mentioned the case of John, who self-identifies as white. This case, although rare, is worthy of further analysis. John was the respondent who was not told that his biological father was black until he was 18, and the information did not change his racial self-understanding whatsoever. In part, John's failure to consider the race of his father as necessitating a modification of his racial identity is due to the negative association with the circumstances of his conception. It is also partly due to his physical appearance and the fact that other people assume, without question, that he is white. In this case, the individual has constructed an identity as white without knowing that his biological father was African American. This identity was consistently validated throughout his socialization. When the critical information was revealed, he was unable to reconcile it with his constructed identity. Instead of questioning his self-understanding or reevaluating the self in light of the new information, this individual chose to have his appearance permanently altered to support his existing racial identity.[39]

The singular understanding of biracial identity typically relies heavily on a combination of physical characteristics and the cultural availability of identity options. For many, the border, protean, and/or transcendent identities are not available either because others do not hold the categories to be meaningful or because their physical appearance demands adherence to traditional categories of racial categorizations.

Of the respondents who adopted a singular black identity, 95.5 percent reported that others "assume they are black." Even when they do not "appear black" and are ambiguous in appearance, others assume they are black, and these assumptions have led most of these individuals to understand themselves as black. In fact, none of those choosing the singular black identity said that they "appear white and could pass," even though 27.3 percent of them described themselves as having light skin color.

In the case of the singular black identity, we see a straightforward relationship between appearance and racial identity. Respondents who chose this identity option overwhelmingly were assumed by other people to be black despite the fact that they described themselves as having a wide range of skin colors. Predictably, the pre-view, program, and review were all black, and the mutual identification process occurred quickly, efficiently, and without incident in the course of social interaction.

Appearance and the Protean Identity

In contrast to both the border and singular identities, some individuals understand their racial identity as characterized by their protean capacity to move between and among cultural contexts and established identities. They understand being biracial as the ability to cross cultural boundaries between black, white, and biracial, which is possible because they possess the ability to present a black, white, and biracial program successfully. These individuals highlighted their cultural savvy in multiple social worlds and understood biracialism as the way in which they were validated, however conditionally, in varied interactional settings. More specifically, these people were accepted as selves with various racial identities by members of different racial groups in diverse social contexts. They believe their dual experiences with both whites and blacks have given them the ability to shift their identity according to the context of any particular interaction and, most important, they have learned to imagine the presentation of self desired by their audience and to adjust their program to that pre-view. This contextual shifting is evidence of a complex self, one that has a heightened concomitant awareness of the self in action.

Individuals who understood being biracial as a protean identity were most likely to use multiple and varied self-labels. At times, they would call themselves black, at other times, white ethnic, and at still other times, biracial. They readily admitted checking different racial identity boxes on institutional forms according to what they thought the audience would find most favorable. For example, when filling out admissions forms for colleges and universities, members of this group admitted checking black as their race. They did so because of a perception that this would enhance their opportunities of gaining admission or financial aid. This example illustrates well the use of programs by this group to manipulate information (albeit in this case, the program is bureaucratic and not put forth in face-to-face interaction). Here, the programs are always false, and the individual putting them forth knows they are false. These programs are false precisely because the individual falls into a location that cannot be easily categorized by appearance. Instead of constant negotiation (the strategy of the border identity), protean respondents put emphasis on playing the expected role, or allowing the pre-view to dictate the program instead of an authentic self. People cannot simply look at them and know that they are black-Irish-biracial or black-German-biracial. Even if it were somehow possible to communicate this in their bodily presence, it would be an ambiguous or meaningless category of understanding for most others. It would not allow for the facile categorization that the general categories of placement provide. In other words, it would not facilitate the important process of mutual identification.

According to our survey data, the skin color of respondents choosing the protean identity is centered in the middle of the phenotype spectrum. In addition, they have a fairly wide range of appearance as understood through the reviews of others; however, most report their appearance as "ambiguous, but assumed black" by others. We are cautious in our interpretation of the appearance-identity link for this identity type because of the small number of survey respondents describing their racial identity as protean. We therefore limit our discussion of the role of appearance in the development of this identity to our analysis of interview data.

Individuals choosing the protean identity option maximized their manipulation of appearance by using secondary and tertiary cues. They moved in and between Standard and Black Vernacular English with an intuitive ease. In one case, we were able to observe this during the interview. The respondent and the interviewer were seated in the main eating area on campus, and several of the respondent's friends approached the table during the interview. The respondent greeted each one differently, some with Standard English and some with Black Vernacular English, some with a stiff body posture, some with a loose demeanor. In fact, due to the ambiguities in the interviewer's appearance, this particular respondent began the interview speaking Standard English because he was unable to assess her pre-view. Several minutes into the interview, he directly inquired about her racial identity. After receiving an answer, his formal demeanor instantly slipped away, and he never again used Standard English.

Renegotiating a program is, for this group, not a fundamentally problematic experience. If, for any reason, their pre-view is wrong or they misjudge the expected response of the other, they simply renegotiate. A challenge to a projected identity is not equivalent to a questioning of the self (although it would be for Stone's definition of self). For those who understand being biracial as a border identity, an unvalidated program would be highly problematic. If, for example, someone were to call an unvalidated border biracial a derogatory name used exclusively for African Americans and the context of the situation did not allow for renegotiation, that person's self-understanding would be directly called into question. For the protean group, however, no such self-questioning would be necessary.

Because they are continually engaged in the concomitant awareness of the pre-view/ program/review process and are not particularly wedded to any one program, they can shift to an alternative program without great social psychological cost.

Appearance and the Transcendent Identity

A small number of our respondents described themselves as having no racial identity (13.8 percent of the survey sample). We have described this final way of understanding biracialism as reminiscent of Robert Park's "Marginal Man" because Park described the qualities of the cosmopolitan stranger as an individual who was bicultural (as opposed to biracial) and whose marginal status enabled an objective view of social reality. The nonracial identity is a transcendent identity because, like Park's stranger, individuals with this self-understanding view their biracialism as placing them in a unique position of marginalization, one that enables an objective perspective of the social meaning placed on race.

The transcendent identity was most prevalent among our interview respondents whose appearance was white. For them, the program put forth was intentionally raceless because they did not consider themselves to have any racial identity whatsoever. Given that American society has a finite codification system of racial group membership, this purported raceless program was the functional equivalent to putting forth a white program. In fact, built into every interaction for these respondents was the anticipation that the reviews of others would be erroneous, or an acceptance of the fact that others would assume they are white. For example, when one respondent entered into an interactional context, his physical features did not in and of themselves announce any particular racial identity (by default, he was considered white). He did not engage in any attempts to use secondary or tertiary cues, such as the purposive use of Black Vernacular English or certain types of apparel, consciously to put forth a program that might hint of any racial group membership. In his mind, he continuously put forth programs that announced various identities that were unrelated to any master-status racial category. Because his bodily features were unambiguous (he looked white), the reviews were consistently mistaken in the assumption of white racial group membership.

This individual allowed the mistaken reviews to facilitate the announcement of his alternative programs, but he would reveal his parentage if the information was requested.

This type of an identity has been constructed over time due to the ambiguity of the individual's appearance and to parental socialization stressing the inaccuracies and ideological problems of racial categorization. Because of his bodily ambiguities, he can go for long periods of time with the nonracial identity maintained, or with his various nonracial programs continuously validated. However, in some social contexts and for some individuals, attempts to avoid, deny, or denounce categorization are unacceptable. It is intolerable in some contexts precisely because the mutual identification process that uses racial categorizations has meaningful consequences. Where racial group membership is a particularly salient feature of everyday life, group membership serves to signify where people will stand on social issues, with whom they can (and cannot) be friends, and the range of others considered acceptable in the dating pool. On entering this type of social context, where the raceless stranger is no longer an available possibility, the demands for self-identification are both persistent and difficult to avoid for those with a transcendent identity.

Given that the one-drop rule remains, by and large, the cultural and legal norm, the result is a grudging acceptance of categorization as black. We refrain from saying that these respondents accept a black *identity* because it is only the label black that is accepted. This particular group of individuals (those transcendents who do not look black) may also find themselves in social contexts where they experience the double bind of not being accepted as black by either whites or blacks.

Of the transcendent survey respondents, only 4.5 percent said they "appear black." Observing that so few respondents appeared black, we felt that our analysis of the interview respondents was substantiated. However, we also wondered about the respondents who simultaneously reported having a transcendent identity and a black appearance. Transcendency, by definition, entails a race-free program. Yet, if individuals appear black to others and are subsequently assumed to be black, how can they espouse a race-free program? More directly, how can individuals feasibly uphold a race-free program if they appear black, when appearing black in and of itself forces race to impinge on daily life?

Those choosing the transcendent option perceive themselves to have no racial identity. Their lack of a racial identity leads them to neither seek nor desire validation of their self-understanding. Because the basis of a transcendent identity is a refusal to participate in a flawed and biologically unsubstantiated system of human categorization, any interaction that would potentially validate or contest a racial identity is meaningless. Put simply, an identity that does not exist cannot be validated. Although we had originally suspected that the transcendent identity option was only available to individuals whose physical appearance was white, our survey data failed to support that assertion. A transcendent identity may be facilitated by a white appearance because of the absurdity of a situation that includes the one-drop rule (mandating a black identity), an individual's appearance (white), and existence in predominately white social networks. However, a white appearance does not determine a transcendent identity, nor is this racial identity option exclusively available to individuals with a white appearance.

In sum, the results indicate there is no association between self-perceived skin color and identity, yet there is a strong association between socially mediated appearance and identity. In addition, we observed a relationship between skin color and appearance. This indicates that appearance mediates the link between skin color and identity. What is less clear is whether or not these three primary associations of interest are affected by contextual experiences of race. Is the relationship between appearance and identity the same for biracials from predominantly black pre-adult contexts? Is the relationship between skin color and identity always insignificant, or does it become important if the biracial person experiences negative treatment from blacks or whites? These are but two questions explored in the final sections of this chapter.

Phenotype and Appearance in Racial Identification Under Differing Contextual Experiences of Race

An individual's social context seems to be a crucial component in the relationship between phenotype and socially perceived appearance and in how these two factors influence identity. Our theoretical framework implies that pre-views and reviews, both of which affect perceived appearance, are socially derived. Biracial individuals, then, integrate these interactional resources into their sense of self, and, as we shall see, their sense of racial identity. Two important ways in which parameters are set for these processes are (a) the influence of the racial composition of significant social networks throughout biracials' socialization (particularly in the pre-adult years) and (b) their experiences of negative treatment from blacks and/or whites.

Is it possible that context influences biracials' perceptions of their own skin color and appearance? Our results indicate that there is an association between biracial people's perceptions of their skin color and the racial composition of their pre-adult socialization contexts. Those biracials who reported having darker skin color came from contexts with more whites, whereas those who perceived their skin color as lighter came from pre-adult contexts of predominantly blacks. This indicates that the racial composition of people's surroundings influences the manner in which they perceive their own skin color. In addition, before looking at the associations of interest and how the racial composition of contexts affects those, it is interesting to note that there is also an association between the racial composition of biracial respondents' pre-adult contexts and their socially mediated appearance. Three findings are most interesting in this regard: biracial people who say they appear white and could "pass" came from predominantly black contexts; those who say they are ambiguous and not assumed black by others were more likely to come from predominantly white contexts; and those who report that they look black and are assumed to be black by others came from predominantly black social networks. These findings should be kept in mind as we consider the influence of context on the associations of interest. In addition, they support our expansion of Stone's model by illustrating that individuals' perceptions and self-understandings are heavily influenced by both their social context and interactional experiences.

Early Contextual Experiences of Race: Racial Composition of Pre-Adult Social Networks

Biracial individuals exist in a variety of social contexts and are socialized by a myriad of agents, some of them black and some of them white (and some themselves biracial). In this final section, we explore how these different contextual experiences of race influence the primary processes of interest in this chapter.

It bears repeating that in our entire sample, regardless of context, there was no association between skin color and identity. This relationship remains insignificant for both predominantly white and integrated contexts. However, there is a significant relationship between skin color and racial identity among biracials who were raised in predominantly black contexts. A closer look at the data reveals that 65 percent of those with darker skin chose a singular black identity , whereas 61.3 percent of those with lighter skin and 57.9 percent of those with medium skin adopted the unvalidated border identity. This means that dark-skinned biracial individuals who grew up in predominantly black contexts developed a singular black identity more than any other identity. Furthermore, those biracial individuals whose skin ranged from light to medium and who were socialized in primarily black contexts were more likely to say that they understand themselves as biracial but they experience the world as a black person. The fact that the relationship between skin color and identity is salient within individuals who grew up in a predominately black pre-adult context may provide support for the idea that the black community sees shades of color whereas whites tend to see only two colors, black and white.

The association between appearance and identity existed for the entire sample of biracials. This association remains regardless of the racial composition of biracials' pre-adult contexts. Thus, the racial composition of biracials' early interactional contexts does not affect the relationship between appearance and identity choices. However, we proposed that these contextual factors would alter this relationship. We predicted that the appearance-identity link would be somewhat stronger or weaker depending on the context. This is in fact the case. The appearance-identity link is strongest in mixed white/black pre-adult contexts. This seems to indicate that these contexts are more complex and more full of a variety of pre-views and reviews that need to be taken into consideration. In fact, within these integrated contexts, (a) 80 percent of those who "appear white and could pass" developed a validated border identity; (b) 40.4 percent of those who are "ambiguous and assumed black" developed an unvalidated border identity; and (c) 68.8 percent of those who "appear black and are assumed black" developed a singular black identity. The appearance-identity link is weakest in predominantly black pre-adult contexts primarily because the border group's experiences and self-understandings are less likely to be validated in predominantly black social networks.

Finally, we have discussed how the association between skin color and appearance for the entire sample was significant. Taking into consideration social context, we find that skin color is not associated with appearance in predominantly white contexts and is most strongly associated with appearance in predominantly black contexts. Again, it appears that the black community can and does distinguish among the variation in skin tones among biracials, whereas whites see only two "colors," black and white. Previous research suggested that this colorism is widely discernible within the black community.[40] We further discuss the implications of these findings in Chapter 6.

Push Factors in Identity: The Experience of Negative Treatment From Blacks and Whites

Most of the biracials in our sample experienced negative treatment from both blacks and whites. We wanted to investigate whether or not this particular contextual experience of race moderates the three associations of interest. Experiencing a push factor of this kind from blacks might lead a biracial of darker skin not to adopt a black identity. On the other hand, a light-skinned biracial who experiences negative treatment from whites may choose to adopt a black identity. We also look at that group of biracials who report experiencing negative treatment from both groups.

As mentioned above, there is no association between skin color and identity for our sample of black/white biracials. However, this relationship does exist for biracials who have experienced negative treatment from blacks, from whites, and from both groups. A closer look at the data illustrates the push factors. Of dark-skinned biracial people who have experienced negative treatment from blacks, 31.4 percent adopt a singular black identity, compared to 42.6 percent of dark-skinned biracials who have experienced such treatment from whites. This kind of contextual experience of race does seem to moderate the appearance-identity association in our data; the association is still significant but stronger in the case of biracials who have experienced negative treatment from whites. The same applies to skin color and appearance.

The extent to which social context influences racial identity formation of biracial respondents remains complicated, but the fact that social context does indeed influence racial identity formation is undeniable.

Discussion

When focusing on master statuses, particularly on racial identity, the use of appearance as a signifier of group membership is not always clear-cut. When we examine mixed-race identities and the relationship between appearance and the choice of identities that individuals make, that relationship becomes even more complex. We have put forth the various types of self-understandings that biracial people have of their racial identity to allow us to explore how the proposed expansion of Stone's model linking appearance and identity development may function. In each of the types of identities, we have attempted to show how the basic processes of mutual identification and concomitant awareness help us better understand two outcomes. The first is how people with the same parental background (one black and one white parent) can make very different choices about their identity(ies). The second is to try to understand why people's appearance does not always predict that outcome— or why we find people who are physically white but identify as black and those who are physically black who say they are *not* black but biracial.

Interpretation of these cases becomes clearer if we focus on the basic processes that take place between individuals and within the individual. That first process of mutual identification is critical to both identity construction and maintenance. If individual actors (regardless of bodily characteristics) exist within a social context where biracial is a meaningful term, they may cultivate a border identity. If this cultural category does not exist and they become accustomed to and adept at switching from black to white, they will cultivate a protean identity. If their appearance is white, they may develop a transcendent identity but only if their social context does not demand categorization. If none of these options is available to an individual, then existing cultural norms dictate racial identity above and beyond (and at times in spite of) their appearance.

The second process at work allows us to see the self functioning as subject. How does the self reflect on its own identity-in-context? In some cases (the protean identity), we saw the self as not only having the capacity for concomitant awareness but using that capacity in all interactions as a survival tool. Individuals were able to assess the anticipated review from the approaching other, to modify the program accordingly, and to continually monitor for necessary renegotiations or reformulations of the program. This intense activity requires an ongoing subjective awareness of the self's activities and much bicultural capital. We see this same process continually at work in the other identity options; however, it takes on a slightly variant form of activity. Simply put, racial identities are subject to a degree of constraint that ethnic identities are not. Specifically, racial identities are constrained by historical stratification that is directly tied to bodily characteristics. It is these characteristics that linger in our cultural symbols and traditional ways of thinking and being. For individuals who are caught in between existing cultural categories at a time of uneven but emerging changes in those categories, appearance remains a significant constraining factor in identity construction and maintenance.

6

Who Is Black Today, and Who Will Be Black Tomorrow?

This book began with a description of the battle that was waged over the possible addition of a multiracial category to the 2000 census. The push for change was led by a coalition of advocacy groups driven by white mothers of biracial children.[1] The multiracial initiative was strongly opposed by leaders of the African American community. Those in favor of the change cited the increasing numbers of mixed-race people in the population and insisted that these people self-identify as biracial. Failing to recognize this emerging group with a separate racial category, advocates argued, was an inaccurate reflection of demographic reality. The opposition contended that historically, traditionally, and culturally society has viewed biracial people, particularly black/white biracials, as black and that these individuals experience the world as black people. Jon Michael Spencer summed up this dilemma by arguing that "there is some tension between having racial categories that serve the legislative and programmatic needs of the federal government and having categories that reflect the self-perceptions of American citizens."[2]

At a broader level, the debate over adding a multiracial category to the census was important because it caused a reexamination of the fundamental question, Who is black in America? Historically, this question has been answered by application of the one-drop rule, meaning that individuals with any black ancestry whatsoever, regardless of their physical appearance, belonged to the black race. The proposition of adding a new category for mixed-race people implied some level of rejection of the one-drop rule and a need for a reassessment of the question, Who is black? as we enter the new millennium.

Because the black-white division is the most salient of all racial dichotomies in the United States, at the center of the controversy is the question of how black/white biracial people understand their racial identity. Both parties in the census debate held the same flawed assumption as the foundation of their positions. They each assumed that biracial people have a singular way in which they understand their racial identity or are understood by others. Multiracial advocates argued that most (if not all) black/white mixed-race people identify as biracial, whereas black leaders argued that this same group of people identifies exclusively as black, in accordance with how society views them. This high-stakes confrontation led both sides to become so deeply entrenched in their own positions that each group used its mutually exclusive, empirically unsubstantiated vision of biracial identity to support its political agenda.

Our findings, presented in the preceding chapters, confirm that neither the multiracial advocates nor black leaders had a complete picture of the complex reality of biracial identity. Our analysis in Chapter 3 revealed that individuals with one black and one white parent have multiple ways in which they understand their racial identity. Some choose a singular identity (either exclusively black or exclusively white); some choose a border identity (which can be either validated or not); others use the protean option of choosing between black, white, or biracial identities at different times and different places; and still others choose the transcendent path, denying any racial identity whatsoever. The most important finding of this study in relation to the census debate is that today among black/white biracial people, there is no singular agreed-on understanding of what it means to be biracial in America.

More important to an overall understanding of the social psychological processes that individuals use to develop and maintain a racial identity are the findings presented in Chapters 4 and 5. Here, we asked how it is possible that people with the same racial background can make radically different choices about their racial identity. We demonstrated that although there are different paths to each identity option, two important social processes govern these choices: social context and interactional validation. Within any social context, biracial people may only choose a racial identity within a range of options that are socially acceptable. Different social networks offer distinct parameters of available identity options among which biracials can select. Within each individual's own, somewhat restrictive range, appearance, socialization, and experiences of rejection or acceptance by both racial groups influence racial identity development. Most important, the responses of others in an actor's social network have the power to validate (or leave unvalidated) any proposed racial identity.

In this final chapter, we consider how variance in racial identity among biracials speaks to the larger questions about the future of the one-drop rule and the ongoing discourse over the question, Who is black in America? To address such salient issues, it is necessary to consider the reality of race and racial categorization and the politics underlying both the challenges and the defenses of that system.

Who Is Black Today?

The United States is certainly not the only society in which multiracial populations have existed. F. James Davis provides an extensive analytic exploration of cross-cultural alternatives used for dealing with racial hybrid groups.[3] Internationally, mixed-race individuals hold various historically and contextually specific statuses relative to other groups in society. In places such as India and Uganda, multiracials' status is lower than the status of either parent group. A mixed-race individual's position in society could also be higher than that of either parent group, as is the case with the mestizos in Mexico. South Africa's "coloureds" illustrate another potential status for multiracial people, in which the individual has a status that is viewed as between that of the parent groups. Yet another possibility is for the individuals' social status to be dependent on nonracial factors, such as education level and wealth, rather than on the race of their parents. This is exemplified in lowland Latin America and most of the Caribbean. Hawaii presents an additional alternative in which mixed-race individuals' social status is perceived as equal to that of all parent groups. Finally, Davis argues, mixed-race people can be an assimilating minority group.[4]

The status of assimilating minority, according to Spencer, is the implied rule for all racial minorities in the United States except African

Americans.[5] In practice, U.S. citizens with one quarter or less Native American, Mexican, Chinese, or Japanese ancestry are treated as assimilating Americans. They are not subjected to the one-drop rule, and their racial background becomes analogous to a symbolic ethnicity. Because of the uniqueness of the one-drop rule in defining who is black, the possibility of being an assimilating minority has been unavailable to African Americans.

The United States has historically followed the pattern of hypodescent, where the mixed-race group has had the same position as the lower-status parent group. In other words, children of black/white interracial unions have been considered black by society and have been accepted within the black community as black. In the context of American history, the one-drop rule has only been eliminated in circumstances where the dominant majority has provided and accepted an alternative racial identity for biracial people. Specifically, the majority group has had the power to set the parameters of available identity options for mixed-race people.[6] Cases of deviance from the one-drop rule have occurred only when whites have allowed biracials to act as a buffer group in support of existing race relations. This was the case for mulattos in Charleston, South Carolina, and New Orleans, Louisiana, prior to the Civil War, and it has not recurred since that time.

The one-drop rule has historically been fully accepted by whites, blacks, and biracial people. Unquestioned acceptance ended when the multiracial movement challenged that norm during the debate over adding a multiracial category to the 2000 census. Interestingly, while the one-drop rule was being contested by multiracial advocates, the group most strongly in favor of maintaining the classification norm was African Americans. The tensions and inherent paradox of blacks being the strongest defenders of the one-drop rule was captured in the following statement made by Davis:

> If one result of such a change would be to cause some lighter colored persons to leave the black community for the white community, the former would lose some of its hard-won political strength, perhaps some of its best leaders, some members of its churches, and other community institutions, some business and professional people, and some customers and clients. American blacks now feel they have an important vested interest in a rule that has for centuries been a key instrument in their oppression.[7]

We suggested in Chapter 1 that underlying the census debate were fundamentally different visions of the future of race relations. Mixed-race identity, for many within the black community, is seen as a transitional identity that, with continued intermarriage, will lead some blacks down the path of assimilation. Total assimilation has long been rejected as a goal within the black community in favor of an egalitarian pluralism. It is worth noting that this rejection of total social integration was a conclusion reluctantly reached by the vast majority of African Americans as a result of continual white resistance. Essentially, the aversion to assimilation was, as Jennifer Hochschild observed, a reaction formation to white rejection.[8] Therefore, blacks experienced a double bind after the passage of civil rights legislation. On one hand, there was encouragement of institutional integration in efforts to reduce economic inequalities and move toward the pluralist dream. On the other hand, white resistance forced black leaders to reject more complete social integration and the eventuality of total assimilation (via intermarriage). Informal sanctions remain strong among both blacks and whites against interracial marriage.[9] The social taboo against intermarriage, which at a deeper level represents a mutual pressure against assimilation, has the effect of reinforcing the one-drop rule. Spencer emphasizes this point:

> So, while whites, with their majority status, hunt down, identify, and discriminate against everyone with that one drop, the greater number of blacks resulting from the rule make it more difficult for our oppressors to maintain the institutions of discrimination. This is no doubt the reason that doing away with the one-drop rule has never been on the civil rights agenda.[10]

Davis has argued that the status of the assimilating minority, is unlikely to occur in the United States because of the persistence of the one-drop rule.[11] Non-black racial groups have typically experienced upward social mobility through intermarriage. When their racial ancestry becomes one fourth or less, they are accepted as assimilated Americans. For example, individuals who are one fourth or less Filipino and three fourths white may be proud of their Filipino ancestry in a way that is similar to someone who is one fourth or less German, Irish, or Italian. In the first and second generation after intermarriage, non-black mixed-race persons may experience some discrimination, but by the fourth generation, their racial identity has become equivalent to the symbolic ethnicity of white ethnics.[12] Blacks, in contrast, have been permanently detoured from the assimilation path because of the one-drop rule and the racism that underlies it. According to the logic of the one-drop rule, no amount of intermarriage or generational distance can remove a person from being categorized as black, or as Gunnar Myrdal points out, "no amount of white ancestry, except one hundred percent, will permit entrance to the white race."[13]

At the conclusion of his lengthy sociohistorical analysis of the one-drop rule as America's answer to the question, Who is black? Davis predicted that "it seems unlikely that the one-drop rule will be modified in the foreseeable future, for such a move would generally be opposed by both whites and blacks."[14] He argues that the only possibility for change lies in the reduction of prejudice and discrimination against African Americans.

Who Will Be Black Tomorrow?

We consider accurate Davis's prediction that the demise of the one-drop rule will not occur without opposition from both blacks and whites and without significant reductions in prejudice and discrimination. Clearly, when we consider the politics underlying the debate over the potential addition of a multiracial category, we see various interest groups whose support for a multiracial category and opposition to it ultimately reify the fallacy of racial categorization.

Throughout this text, we have used the terms white and black to designate racial groups as if they represent biologically real categorizations. In trying to address the question of who is black, we must first and foremost recognize that the logic of racial classification is predicated on the idea that racial groups are pure and discrete groupings of human beings. Categorization implies the existence of mutually exclusive, biologically identifiable groups. However, social scientists agree that racial groupings are not based in biological reality. Halford Fairchild summarized the arguments against racial classification by stating,

> The arguments against the validity of the concept of race are as follows: (a) it is an ideological invention that supported European and American imperialism; (b) the definition of race as a reproductively isolated group (one that has unique phenotypic characteristics results in thousands of

races, not three; (c) within each of the three "racial" groups, the variation in attributes and characteristics exceeds the average between-group differences; and (d) "racial" classification ignores the overwhelming commonality in the genetic histories of homo sapiens, and this biological evidence points to one race, not three or thousands.[15]

Race, and therefore racial categorization as it is commonly understood, is simply not a biological reality. Because race is a social delusion, it requires an elaborate set of rules and regulations to maintain. These rules, of course, would be unnecessary if it were biologically real. Knowing that pure races are nonexistent, separating individuals into fictional categories becomes a problematic task, fraught with inconsistencies.

Racial categorization becomes even more difficult when we consider that race as a biological fact is not real, although race as a social construct is. Although structural barriers have decreased since the passage of civil rights legislation, African Americans continue to experience residential segregation, educational inequalities, and discrimination in the housing market, criminal justice system, and labor market. In addition to basic institutional inequalities, race also continues to affect the way individuals perceive each other and their social interactions on a daily basis. As Heather Dalmage pointedly states, "while there may be one [human] race, only some members of that race can catch a cab on 42nd street."[16] In this way, the biologically unreal becomes socially real in the context of daily interactions and institutional structure. It is this social reality of race that leads civil rights leaders to argue that census categorization is inherently a political designation.

Truly, racial categorization is a quandary. On one hand, racial categories are biologically baseless. On the other hand, race affects the most basic of daily interactions and individual opportunities. In this context, the multiracial movement's challenge to the census can be seen as cutting into the core of that paradox and shining a light on one of our deepest social problems. On the surface, the coalition of groups in the multiracial movement challenged one of the key rules to racial classification in the United States, the one-drop rule. At a deeper level, they challenged the key pillar of purity and mutual exclusivity underlying the entire project of racial classification. The potential addition of the multiracial category, while questioning the system, has the simultaneous effect of reifying that very system. If, in fact, multiracial activists believe that race is a meaningless social construct, then it is senseless to add a modification to a meaningless system. In other words, the quest to add an additional category only makes the existing categories seem even more real. Kwame Anthony Appiah made this critique: "[The] multiracial scheme, which is meant to solve anomalies, simply creates more anomalies of its own, and that's because the fundamental concept—that you should be able to assign every American to one of three or four races reliably—is crazy."[17] This separate status also inflames long-standing resentments within the African American community because mobilizing for a separate category also suggests that individuals do indeed want to separate themselves from traditional communities of color.

The debate proceeded in accordance with Davis's prediction. Black leaders, who were focused on social justice and resource allocation, viewed race as a political construct that is a real constraint in the lives and experiences of people of color. Multiracial advocates requested a multiracial category, further reifying the reality of this unreal concept. However, one development that Davis may not have predicted was the support of white conservatives who supported the multiracial movement. This backing was predicated on the idea that a multiracial category was a first step toward the destruction of all racial categories. In fact, Newt Gingrich was quoted as stating, "I believe that we can begin to address the country's racial divide by adding a multiracial category to federal forms and the United States Census while simultaneously phasing out the outdated, divisive and rigid classification of Americans" and "ultimately, our goal is to have one classification—American."[18] This coalition between some groups within the multiracial coalition and conservative politicians was based on an ideology of color blindness; it asserts that if racial categories are unreal (in their biological foundation), then the appropriate response would ultimately be to eliminate all categorizations. This position negates the social reality of race by denying the continued existence of racial inequalities. The spectacle of Susan Graham (a white mother of biracial children and director of Project RACE) and Newt Gingrich (the personification of the conservative right) joining forces to call for the ultimate dismantling of all racial categorization confirmed the worst fears of civil rights leaders, who saw the multiracial movement being used as a tool to dismantle civil rights gains by stripping the government of the capacity to enforce that legislation. The paradox, of course, is that the extreme position of calling for an end to racial categorization represents the only real challenge to the fiction of racial groupings made by multiracial activists, and it was this position that was embraced by conservative whites.

And so, the debate over the multiracial category mirrored the reality of how race is lived in America. Race continues to be simultaneously a biological fallacy and a social reality that defines the distribution of resources and our everyday interactions. We began this project with the assumption that what was missing from the census debate was empirical evidence documenting how multiracial people articulate their reality. In this final section, we return to our biracial respondents to understand how their existence, which is most contested in this debate, provides answers to the question of who is black in America.

Who Will Be Black in 2010?

Drawing on our analysis, several important facts about racial identity emerge. First, what it is *not*: racial identity is not fixed, rigid, or codifiable. It is not based on personal, individualistic choices. It is not mutually exclusive, nor is it deterministic. We have learned however, that racial identity is malleable, rooted in both macro and micro social processes, and that it has structurally and culturally defined parameters. In short, our work supports the long-standing sociological assertion that race is a socially constructed reality, one that has changed, and continues to change, over time.

Each of the four identity groups has something to offer to an understanding of the mixed-race experience. Thus, it becomes clear that each of the identity types—strategies that grew out of negotiating an identity as a black/white biracial in a society enamored with a biological and phenotypic understanding of race—provides some answer to the question of who is black in the United States.

Those individuals who understand themselves racially as what we have termed the validated border identity represent multiracial advocates' idealized and preferred notion of mixed-race people's resolution of the marginal status that they hold in our society.[19] They no longer perform the juggling act that straddling the color line in the United States would seem to necessitate for black/white biracials. Their self-understanding as exclusively biracial has been validated by others within their interactional spheres throughout their lives. As mentioned in previous chapters, validation is only available when other members of a social network hold the identity option as one of the possibilities for individuals of mixed-race ancestry to adopt. It is this group of biracials, those with a validated border identity, that has spawned the advocacy wing of the debate over racial classification. Its members appear to supply the strongest platform from which to argue the need for a new category of racial classification—if the category exists, so does the possibility of achieving validation for a person's identity.

There is, of course, another side to the story given to us by those identifying as exclusively biracial: the experience of the unvalidated border identity. This group illuminates for us the very fact that individuals can understand themselves in one way, yet fail to have that classification accepted by others. This failure to have biracial accepted as a legitimate category of identity complicates the issues raised by the validated biracials. First, it could be the case that if the category of multiracial existed in Americans' cultural lexicon, then those who understood themselves as borders would be more likely to be validated by others in interaction. However, another possibility, which the unvalidated narrative illustrates for us, is that current racial categories, in and of themselves, and the stereotypes and assumptions they carry with them, are antithetical to the validation of emergent racial identities. Adding a multiracial category could allow people to adopt an identity that does not currently exist in the U.S. racial classification scheme, presuming that others will accept this category as fully as they do the standing categories.

Some black/white biracials choose to identify themselves racially in alliance with one of their birth parents. Another way to see those who choose a singular identity is to acknowledge the resolution of their marginality through an identification *with* or an identification *away from* one of the traditional racially categorized social groups, blacks or whites. Even though this choice—the singular black identity—has been the expected identity of choice for black/white biracials, our findings suggest that the choice to identify with one or the other racial background is extremely complex and is grounded in several processes: (a) group reference, (b) socialization into one of the groups, and (c) a variety of interactional push and pull factors. Physical appearance plays an important role in singular identity choices, yet in modes that interact with these other processes in unexpected and complicated ways. Those adopting a singular identity illuminate for us the fact that although we may discuss race and racial categorization as socially constructed, the lived reality is that race has serious implications for people's lives and opportunities.

Living within a marginal space presents identity choices for most black/white biracial individuals. For some, however, racial identity does not revolve around making choices but requires paying strict attention to the multiplicity of social contexts and cultural schemas within which that person exists. At the same time, it is both necessary and desirable to build repertoires from all angles to experience the complexity of their status fully. In this sense, those choosing the protean identity straddle socially constructed racial categories, learning the ins and outs of various social worlds and moving freely and fluidly among them. This identity choice effectively shows us that the black, white, and biracial "worlds" are different but that it is possible to coexist effectively and constructively within these networks and to understand the reality of American life with all its diversity.

The final group we wish to discuss is the transcendents. This group is exceedingly important to acknowledge because their resolution of the biracial dilemma is a refusal to participate in the fallacy of race, whether in its monoracial, multiracial, or biracial manifestations. From their perspective, the system of racial classification, the trinity of color-race-identity, and the hierarchical valuation of racial identities are damaging and fundamentally problematic. At the same time, they are cognizant of the existence of racial inequalities. Some may comprehend these inequalities only intellectually because of their white appearance, whereas others experience racism directly in their daily existence. Their marginality has allowed them to take an objective stance on race and denounce it as useless. Transcendents understand themselves as human—nothing more and certainly nothing less. If the transcendents composed the bulk of the movement for a change in the 2010 census categories, they would dismantle them completely and thoroughly but not without explaining why they would do so and why categorization is damaging to the human experience and, most important, not without considering the effects of such a move on civil rights compliance and monitoring via existing categories.

In the final analysis, the one-drop rule seems headed for a slow and painful death. The plurality of racial identity options chosen by biracial people, as documented in this book, illustrates the fruitless nature of attempting to capture racial identity in a singular category. In short, although our respondents had the same racial background, they would choose black, white, multiracial, "other," nothing, and variations of all of the above, on forms. None of their replies would provide the information that was being sought. At the same time, the experiences of biracial people in our sample (especially their experiences of discrimination) illustrate for us the continued need to keep racial data.

Affording respondents the option to check all categories that apply was one step forward in acknowledging the fluidity of race and racial categorization. The subsequent decision that multiracial responses would be collapsed back into the traditional five for bureaucratic reasons is a step backward. This awkward dance illustrates perfectly the existing status of race as both real and unreal in American society. More important, although movement has taken place, we continue to stand still as prisoners of the man-made concept of race and the group inequities it has created. Thus, we remain captives of cruel delusion we are as yet unable to escape, acknowledging that our society remains unready for such a move.

Although the efforts of the multiracial movement in the latest round of census modifications were only partially successful, they gained broad recognition and continued support from whites. The multiracial movement will be fought every step of the way by leaders of the black community, for whom the multiracial agenda is a direct and immediate threat at both the practical and ideological levels. One thing remains certain: The answer to the question, Who is black in America? will continue to reflect the deep complexity and issues of power that underlie U.S. race relations.

Appendix A

Open-Ended Interview Questions

(Phase 1: In-depth Interviews)

1. At what age did you become conscious of race?
2. Can you tell me about any memorable experiences you had growing up when you first became aware of race?
3. Was the topic of race explicitly dealt with in your family?
4. Did your parents try to shape your racial identity or tell you how to identify yourself?
5. How would you describe your friendship groups growing up?
6. Did you have friends who were mixed-race? Did you talk about being biracial with each other?
7. What types of names, either positive or negative, can you remember people calling you (both white people and black people)?
8. What was the race of your significant others?
9. Can you remember times in your school experiences when you were very conscious of being your race?
10. How do you describe your racial identity at this time in your life?
11. How did you racially identify yourself on your admissions form?
12. Has the way you understand your racial identity ever changed?
13. Is it more or less important now that you are in college to identify yourself as black/white/or biracial?
14. If you attended a historically black college like [examples], do you think that you would continue to identify yourself as biracial? Do you think that identity would be as easily recognized/accepted there as it is here at [college name]?
15. Describe your current friendship groups?
16. Can you tell me how people typically react to you? What do they assume about your racial identity?
17. Have you ever been to a tanning salon?
18. Have you ever tried to make yourself look (physically) more or less black or white?
19. Do you think that you act differently around black people than white people? What about when you are with your black friends versus when you're with white friends?
20. How do you feel about the idea of a mixed-race category on the census?

21. What do you usually fill out on forms?
22. What do you think that "passing" means for multiracial people?
23. How would you respond to a person who opposes adding a multiracial census category, or the general idea of biracial people identifying themselves as biracial instead of black, by saying that biracial people who do that are in a state of denial?
24. Do you feel like being biracial is an advantage, a disadvantage, or has no meaning in your life?

Appendix B

Written Consent Form

(Phase 1: In-depth Interviews)

You are being asked to participate in a study of racial identity. We hope to learn what it means to have one black and one white parent in the United States and what experiences have influenced your understanding of your racial identity. You were selected as a participant in the interview phase of this study because you have one black and one white biological parent and because you indicated a willingness to be interviewed.

As part of this study, you are being asked to participate in one in-depth interview that will last between one and three hours. During the course of the interview, I will ask you questions that will invite you to recount the unique personal experiences that led to your current self-understanding. Each interview will be audiotaped and later transcribed. If you wish, you may receive a copy of the transcript. I will also take your picture at the end of the interview.

Any information that is obtained in connection with this study and that can be identified with you will remain confidential. Your name will not be used at any time nor will any information that could identify you.

Your decision whether or not to participate will not prejudice your future relations with the [participating colleges and universities]. If you decide to participate, you may withdraw from the interview process at any time. You may withdraw your consent to have specific excerpts used, if you notify the interviewer. If we want to use any materials in any way not consistent with what is stated above, we would ask for your additional written consent.

If you have any questions, we encourage you to ask us. If you have any additional questions later, Kerry Ann Rockquemore [phone number] will be happy to answer them.

You will be given a copy of this form to keep.

YOU ARE MAKING A DECISION WHETHER OR NOT TO PARTICIPATE. YOUR SIGNATURE INDICATES THAT YOU HAVE DECIDED TO PARTICIPATE HAVING READ THE INFORMATION PROVIDED ABOVE.

_____   _____
Signature of participant   Date

_____   _____
Signature of interviewer   Date

Appendix C

Bill of Rights for Racially Mixed People

By Maria Root

(Phase 1: In-depth Interviews)

I HAVE THE RIGHT . . .
Not to justify my existence in this world.
Not to keep the races separate within me.
Not to be responsible for people's discomfort with my physical ambiguity.
Not to justify my ethnic legitimacy.

I HAVE THE RIGHT . . .
To identify myself differently than strangers expect me to identify.
To identify myself differently from how my parents identify me.
To identify myself differently from my brothers and sisters.
To identify myself differently in different situations.

I HAVE THE RIGHT . . .
To create a vocabulary to communicate about being multiracial.
To change my identity over my lifetime—and more than once.
To have loyalties and identification with more than one group of people.
To freely choose whom I befriend and love.

NOTE: The Bill of Rights is taken from Maria Root, Ed., *The Multiracial Experience: Racial Borders as the New Frontier* (Sage, 1996). Reprinted with permission.

Appendix D

Demographic Questionnaire

(Phase 1: In-depth Interviews)

1. Name: _____

2. Age: _____

3. Sex: _____

4. City and State of Birth: _____

5. Race of your parents:

   Mother: _____
   Father: _____

6. Are your parents currently married, separated, divorced, or were they never married? _____

7. What would you estimate is their yearly income? _____

8. Would you describe your elementary school as mostly white, mostly black, or something else? _____

9. Would you describe your high school as mostly white, mostly black, or something else? _____

10. What type of area was the neighborhood you grew up in: urban, suburban, small town, or rural? _____

11. Would you describe your family's neighborhood as mostly white, mostly black, or something else? _____

12. Would you describe the contact you had with your mother's family as frequent, infrequent, or no contact? _____

13. Would you describe the contact you had with your father's family as frequent, infrequent, or no contact? _____

Appendix E

Solicitation Letter

(Phase 2: Mail Survey)

Dear Student,

Over the past two years, researchers at the [college and university names] have been collectively engaged in a study of the social determinants of racial identity among college students. You have been selected as a potential participant in the next stage of this study. The purpose of the study is to address the lack of information on racial identity formation that focuses on individuals who have one black and one non-black parent.

You are one of 4,000 African American college students from the [participating colleges and universities] that we have selected as potential participants in the study. We are hoping to contact as many students as possible with one black and one non-black parent. Our goal is to assemble the largest existing data set of mixed-race college students that will enable a greater understanding of racial identity formation. If you fit this criterion and would be willing to respond to our brief survey, please fill out the enclosed blue reply card and return it at your earliest convenience. If you do not fit this criterion, but know someone else who does, please feel free to pass this information along. Your participation is very important and greatly appreciated.

Once we receive the enclosed reply card, we will send you a survey that takes approximately 15 minutes to complete. A postage paid response envelope will be enclosed for your convenience. We believe our research findings may be of great personal interest to you. Therefore, we will send you a report with our findings at your request.

If you have any questions about the study, or if you would like any additional information, please feel free to contact Kerry Rockquemore at [phone number] or by electronic mail at [e-mail address].

Thank you for taking the time to consider participating in this valuable research project. We look forward to receiving your reply card.

Sincerely,
Kerry A. Rockquemore, Research Director

Appendix F

Survey of Biracial Experiences

(Phase 2: Mail Survey)

1. What is the highest level of education you have completed? (CIRCLE ONE)
   A) High School
   B) Associate's Degree
   C) Bachelor's Degree
   D) Master's Degree
   E) Ph.D.
   F) Other, please specify _____

2. What is the highest level of education you expect to complete? (CIRCLE ONE)
   A) High School
   B) Associate's Degree
   C) Bachelor's Degree
   D) Master's Degree
   E) Ph.D.
   F) Other, please specify _____

3. What is your current occupation? _____

4. What is your date of birth? _____

5. What is the city and state in which you were born? _____

6. Are you male or female? (CHECK ONE) ( ) Male ( ) Female

7. Were you adopted? ( ) Yes ( ) No

8. What is your racial or ethnic origin?
   _____ American Indian/Alaskan Native
   _____ Asian/Pacific Islander
   _____ Black
   _____ Hispanic
   _____ White
   _____ Other _____
   _____ Mixed Race (check all that apply)

_____ American Indian/Alaskan Native
_____ Asian/Pacific Islander
_____ Black
_____ Hispanic
_____ White
_____ Other _____

9. What is your mother's racial or ethnic origin?
_____ American Indian/Alaskan Native
_____ Asian/Pacific Islander
_____ Black
_____ Hispanic
_____ White
_____ Other _____
_____ Mixed Race (check all that apply)
     _____ American Indian/Alaskan Native
     _____ Asian/Pacific Islander
     _____ Black
     _____ Hispanic
     _____ White
     _____ Other _____

10. What is the highest level of education your mother has completed? (CIRCLE ONE)
A) High School
B) Associate's Degree
C) Bachelor's Degree
D) Master's Degree
E) Ph.D.
F) Other, please specify _____

11. When you were growing up, what was your mother's occupation?

_____

12. What is your father's racial or ethnic origin?
_____ American Indian/Alaskan Native
_____ Asian/Pacific Islander
_____ Black
_____ Hispanic
_____ White
_____ Other _____
_____ Mixed Race (check all that apply)

_____ American Indian/Alaskan Native
_____ Asian/Pacific Islander
_____ Black
_____ Hispanic
_____ White
_____ Other _____

13. What is the highest level of education your father has completed? (CIRCLE ONE)
    A) High School
    B) Associate's Degree
    C) Bachelor's Degree
    D) Master's Degree
    E) Ph.D.
    F) Other, please specify _____

14. When you were growing up, what was your father's occupation?
    _____

15. Are your parents currently married to each other? ( ) Yes ( ) No

16. The Census bureau has considered adding a multiracial category to its racial classification system. Which of the following statements would best describe your opinion of that change. (CIRCLE ONE)
    A) I think it is a bad idea because it will have negative effects on the black community.
    B) I think it is a bad idea because it will separate biracial people from blacks.
    C) I think it is a good idea because biracial people should have the opportunity to choose how they want to identify.
    D) I think it is a good idea because it reflects reality within the black population.
    E) I have no opinion.

17. Interracial marriages are currently on the rise in the United States. Which of the following statements best describes your opinion about the children of those unions:
    A) They are black and should identify themselves that way.
    B) They are biracial, but they should identify themselves as black.
    C) They are biracial and should identify themselves that way.
    D) They shouldn't have to define themselves as any one race.
    E) They are biracial, but they should have a choice of how they may identify themselves (as black, biracial, or white).
    F) Other _____

18. Circle the area on the continuum that best describes your skin color?

Black	Dark Brown	Medium Brown	Light Brown	Yellow	Olive	White

19. What was the racial composition of your grammar or elementary school?
( ) All blacks
( ) Mostly blacks
( ) About half black
( ) Mostly whites
( ) All whites
( ) Other

20. What was the racial composition of your closest friends in grammar or elementary school?
( ) All blacks
( ) Mostly blacks
( ) About half black
( ) Mostly whites
( ) All whites
( ) Other

21. What was the racial composition of your junior high school?
( ) All blacks
( ) Mostly blacks
( ) About half black
( ) Mostly whites
( ) All whites
( ) Other

22. What was the racial composition of your high school?
( ) All blacks
( ) Mostly blacks
( ) About half black
( ) Mostly whites
( ) All whites
( ) Other

23. What was the racial composition of your closest friends in high school?
( ) All blacks
( ) Mostly blacks
( ) About half black
( ) Mostly whites
( ) All whites
( ) Other

24. What was the racial composition of your neighborhood while growing up?
( ) All blacks
( ) Mostly blacks
( ) About half black
( ) Mostly whites
( ) All whites
( ) Other

25. What is the racial composition of your college?
( ) All blacks
( ) Mostly blacks
( ) About half black
( ) Mostly whites
( ) All whites
( ) Other

26. What is the racial composition of your present neighborhood?
( ) All blacks
( ) Mostly blacks
( ) About half black
( ) Mostly whites
( ) All whites
( ) Other

27. What is the racial composition of your church or place of worship?
( ) All blacks
( ) Mostly blacks
( ) About half black
( ) Mostly whites
( ) All whites
( ) Other

28. What is the racial composition of your present workplace?
( ) All blacks
( ) Mostly blacks
( ) About half black
( ) Mostly whites
( ) All whites
( ) Other

29. What is the racial composition of your closest friends today?
( ) All blacks
( ) Mostly blacks
( ) About half black
( ) Mostly whites
( ) All whites
( ) Other

30. What is the race of your current, or most recent, significant other (i.e., spouse, love interest, boy/girlfriend)?
_____ American Indian/Alaskan Native
_____ Asian/Pacific Islander
_____ Black
_____ Hispanic
_____ White
_____ Other _____

31. Some people call the slang that African American people speak Black Vernacular or Ebonics. In your home, how would you characterize the use of Black Vernacular?
A) Everyone in my home speaks in the vernacular all the time.
B) We sometimes speak in vernacular, sometime we use Standard English.
C) Standard English is exclusively used in our home.
D) I have never paid attention to the way people speak.
E) Other_____

32. How close do you feel to poor blacks?
( ) Very close
( ) Close
( ) Not close at all

33. How close do you feel to religious blacks?
( ) Very close
( ) Close
( ) Not close at all

34. How close do you feel to young blacks?
( ) Very close
( ) Close
( ) Not close at all

35. How close do you feel to middle-class blacks?
    ( ) Very close
    ( ) Close
    ( ) Not close at all

36. How close do you feel to working-class blacks?
    ( ) Very close
    ( ) Close
    ( ) Not close at all

37. How close do you feel to older blacks?
    ( ) Very close
    ( ) Close
    ( ) Not close at all

38. How close do you feel to blacks with a white parent?
    ( ) Very close
    ( ) Close
    ( ) Not close at all

39. How close do you feel to black elected officials?
    ( ) Very close
    ( ) Close
    ( ) Not close at all

40. How close do you feel to black professionals?
    ( ) Very close
    ( ) Close
    ( ) Not close at all

41. How close do you feel to black entertainers?
    ( ) Very close
    ( ) Close
    ( ) Not close at all

42. How close do you feel to black athletes?
    ( ) Very close
    ( ) Close
    ( ) Not close at all

43. How close do you feel to poor whites?
   ( ) Very close
   ( ) Close
   ( ) Not close at all

44. How close do you feel to religious whites?
   ( ) Very close
   ( ) Close
   ( ) Not close at all

45. How close do you feel to young whites?
   ( ) Very close
   ( ) Close
   ( ) Not close at all

46. How close do you feel to middle-class whites?
   ( ) Very close
   ( ) Close
   ( ) Not close at all

47. How close do you feel to working-class whites?
   ( ) Very close
   ( ) Close
   ( ) Not close at all

48. How close do you feel to older whites?
   ( ) Very close
   ( ) Close
   ( ) Not close at all

49. How close do you feel to white politicians?
   ( ) Very close
   ( ) Close
   ( ) Not close at all

50. How close do you feel to white professionals?
   ( ) Very close
   ( ) Close
   ( ) Not close at all

51. How close do you feel to white entertainers?
    ( ) Very close
    ( ) Close
    ( ) Not close at all

52. How close do you feel to white athletes?
    ( ) Very close
    ( ) Close
    ( ) Not close at all

53. In the neighborhood that you grew up in, the most common language usage was which of the following?
    A) Everyone in my home speaks in the vernacular all the time.
    B) We sometimes speak in vernacular, sometime we use Standard English.
    C) Standard English is exclusively used in our home.
    D) I have never paid attention to the way people speak.

54. Did your parent(s) belong to any race-based political organizations (for example, the NAACP or Urban League)?
    ( ) Yes   ( ) No   ( ) Don't Know

55. Did your parent(s) ever participate in any of the following political activities? (CHECK ALL THAT APPLY)
    ( ) march or demonstration
    ( ) voter drive
    ( ) circulate a petition
    ( ) attend a protest meeting
    ( ) boycott
    ( ) Other _____

56. Did your parent(s) ever discuss personal experiences of discrimination based upon their race/ethnicity?
    ( ) Yes   ( ) No

57. Black children should learn an African language.
    ( ) Strongly agree
    ( ) Agree
    ( ) No opinion
    ( ) Disagree
    ( ) Strongly disagree

58. Blacks should always vote for black candidates when possible.
   ( ) Strongly agree
   ( ) Agree
   ( ) No opinion
   ( ) Disagree
   ( ) Strongly disagree

59. Black women should not date white men.
   ( ) Strongly agree
   ( ) Agree
   ( ) No opinion
   ( ) Disagree
   ( ) Strongly disagree

60. Black people should shop in black-owned shops whenever possible.
   ( ) Strongly agree
   ( ) Agree
   ( ) No opinion
   ( ) Disagree
   ( ) Strongly disagree

61. Black men should not date white women.
   ( ) Strongly agree
   ( ) Agree
   ( ) No opinion
   ( ) Disagree
   ( ) Strongly disagree

62. Black parents should give their children African names.
   ( ) Strongly agree
   ( ) Agree
   ( ) No opinion
   ( ) Disagree
   ( ) Strongly disagree

63. Some parents attempt to influence their children's dating partners. When you think about your own parents, how would you describe their involvement in your choice of dating partners?
   A) They never tried to influence my choice of dating partners.
   B) They tried to influence my dating partners, but it had nothing to do with the person's race.
   C) They tried to influence my dating partners by urging me to date only within my race.
   D) They forbid me from dating outside my race.
   E) Other _____

64. Have you ever experienced personal discrimination or hostility from whites because of your race?
( ) Yes, I have frequently experienced racial discrimination.
( ) Yes, I have occasionally experienced racial discrimination.
( ) No, I have never experienced racial discrimination.

65. Have you ever experienced negative treatment from blacks because of your skin color or physical features?
( ) Yes, I have frequently experienced negative treatment because of my physical appearance.
( ) Yes, I have occasionally experienced negative treatment because of my physical appearance.
( ) No, I have never experienced negative treatment because of my physical appearance.

66. Has anyone ever told you that you talk, dress, or act "white"?
( ) Yes   ( ) No

67. Do you belong to any race-specific organizations or clubs (for example, a black fraternity or sorority or a black student group)?
( ) Yes   ( ) No

68. Have you ever, at any time in the past, belonged to any race-specific organizations or clubs (for example, a black fraternity or sorority or a black student group)?
( ) Yes   ( ) No

69. Individuals have many different types of identities. How would you describe your identity in the following contexts?

I consider my social identity as:
( ) Black
( ) Biracial
( ) White
( ) Other _____

70. I consider my political identity as:
( ) Black
( ) Biracial
( ) White
( ) Other _____

71. I consider my cultural identity as:
    ( ) Black
    ( ) Biracial
    ( ) White
    ( ) Other _____

72. I consider my physical identity as:
    ( ) Black
    ( ) Biracial
    ( ) White
    ( ) Other _____

73. On forms I identify myself as:
    ( ) Black
    ( ) Biracial
    ( ) White
    ( ) Other _____

74. Did you talk openly in your family about being biracial?
    ( ) Yes   ( ) No

75. Did your parents try to directly shape your racial identity?
    ( ) Yes   ( ) No

76. If yes, which racial identity did they encourage you to adopt?
    _____ American Indian/Alaskan Native
    _____ Asian/Pacific Islander
    _____ Black
    _____ Hispanic
    _____ White
    _____ Other _____
    _____ Mixed Race

77. How true do you think it is that most black people are hard working?
    ( ) True   ( ) Somewhat True   ( ) A Little True   ( ) Not True at All

78. How true do you think it is that most black people love their families?
    ( ) True   ( ) Somewhat True   ( ) A Little True   ( ) Not True at All

79. How true do you think it is that most black people are ashamed?
    ( ) True   ( ) Somewhat True   ( ) A Little True   ( ) Not True at All

80. How true do you think it is that most black people are lazy?
( ) True   ( ) Somewhat True   ( ) A Little True   ( ) Not True at All

81. How true do you think it is that most black people neglect their families?
( ) True   ( ) Somewhat True   ( ) A Little True   ( ) Not True at All

82. How true do you think it is that most black people are lying and trifling?
( ) True   ( ) Somewhat True   ( ) A Little True   ( ) Not True at All

83. How true do you think it is that most black people keep trying?
( ) True   ( ) Somewhat True   ( ) A Little True   ( ) Not True at All

84. How true do you think it is that most black people do for others?
( ) True   ( ) Somewhat True   ( ) A Little True   ( ) Not True at All

85. How true do you think it is that most black people give up easily?
( ) True   ( ) Somewhat True   ( ) A Little True   ( ) Not True at All

86. How true do you think it is that most black people are weak?
( ) True   ( ) Somewhat True   ( ) A Little True   ( ) Not True at All

87. How true do you think it is that most black people are proud of themselves?
( ) True   ( ) Somewhat True   ( ) A Little True   ( ) Not True at All

88. How true do you think it is that most black people are honest?
( ) True   ( ) Somewhat True   ( ) A Little True   ( ) Not True at All

89. How true do you think it is that most black people are selfish?
( ) True   ( ) Somewhat True   ( ) A Little True   ( ) Not True at All

90. How true do you think it is that most black people are strong?
( ) True   ( ) Somewhat True   ( ) A Little True   ( ) Not True at All

91. The contact you had with your mother's family (grandparents, aunts, uncles) can be described as:
( ) Daily
( ) Once a week
( ) Once a month
( ) Several times a year
( ) No contact

92. The contact you had with your father's family can be described as:
( ) Daily
( ) Once a week
( ) Once a month
( ) Several times a year
( ) No contact

93. Which of the following responses do you think best describes what your parents taught you about what it is to be (half) black?
A) Be yourself, just take care of yourself.
B) Don't be prejudiced.
C) Whites believe they are superior.
D) None of the above.
E) Other _____

94. Which of the following responses do you think best characterizes the way that your parents taught you about black-white relations?
A) You're as good as anybody else.
B) Recognize that all races are equal.
C) Blacks don't have the chances that whites have.
D) None of the above.
E) Other _____

95. Which of the following responses do you think best describes what your parents taught you about how to get along with white people?
A) Don't ever put your trust in whites.
B) Just work hard.
C) Treat whites the way you want to be treated.
D) None of the above.
E) Other _____

96. What group of people would you say you feel most comfortable being around:
A) I am most comfortable with blacks.
B) I am most comfortable with whites.
C) I am equally comfortable with blacks and whites.
D) I am most comfortable with biracial or multiethnic people.
E) I am most comfortable in diverse groups with people of varying races and ethnicities.
F) Race is not the most important factor that determines my comfort level.

97. Which of the following statements best describes how you feel about your racial identity?
  A) I consider myself exclusively black (or African American).
  B) I sometimes consider myself black, sometimes my other race, and sometimes biracial depending on the circumstances.
  C) I consider myself biracial, but I experience the world as a black person.
  D) I consider myself exclusively biracial (neither black nor white).
  E) I consider myself exclusively my other race (not black or biracial).
  F) Race is meaningless, I do not believe in racial identities.
  G) Other _____

98. Which of the following best describes your physical appearance:
  A) I look black and most people assume that I am black.
  B) My physical features are ambiguous, people assume I am black mixed with something else.
  C) My physical features are ambiguous, people do not assume that I am black.
  D) I physically look white, I could "pass."

99. Have you experienced negative treatment by blacks because you have parents of different races?
  ( ) Yes, I have frequently experienced negative treatment by blacks.
  ( ) Yes, I have occasionally experienced negative treatment by blacks.
  ( ) No, I have never experienced negative treatment by blacks.

100. Have you experienced negative treatment by whites because you have parents of different races?
  ( ) Yes, I have frequently experienced negative treatment by whites.
  ( ) Yes, I have occasionally experienced negative treatment by whites.
  ( ) No, I have never experienced negative treatment by whites.

101. Which of the following positions do you support about the U.S. census racial categorizations?
  ( ) No change should be made in the existing census categories.
  ( ) They should add a multiracial category.
  ( ) They should allow people to "check all that apply" of the existing categories.
  ( ) They should add a multiracial category that allows an individual to "check all that apply" underneath.

102. It is extremely difficult to record many aspects of the biracial experience in a survey. Therefore, would you be willing to be contacted for a brief interview?
( ) Yes   ( ) No

If yes, please provide the following contact information

Name:

_____

Address:

_____

City/State/Zip:

_____

Phone:

_____

Appendix G

Written Consent Form

(Phase 3: In-depth Interviews)

You are being asked to participate in a study of racial identity. We hope to learn what it means to have one black and one white parent in the United States and what experiences have influenced your understanding of your racial identity. You were selected as a participant in the interview phase of this study because you have one black and one white biological parent and because you indicated a willingness to be interviewed on your returned questionnaire.

As part of this study, you are being asked to participate in one in-depth interview that will last between one and three hours. During the course of the interview, I will ask you questions that will invite you to recount the unique personal experiences that led to your current self-understanding. Each interview will be audiotaped and later transcribed. If you wish, you may receive a copy of the transcript. I will also take your picture at the end of the interview.

Any information that is obtained in connection with this study and that can be identified with you will remain confidential. Your name will not be used at any time nor will any information that could identify you.

Your decision whether or not to participate will not prejudice your future relations with the [participating colleges and universities]. If you decide to participate, you may withdraw from the interview process at any time. You may withdraw your consent to have specific excerpts used, if you notify the interviewer. If we want to use any materials in any way not consistent with what is stated above, we would ask for you additional written consent.

If you have any questions, we encourage you to ask us. If you have any additional questions later, Kerry Ann Rockquemore [phone number] will be happy to answer them.

You will be given a copy of this form to keep.

YOU ARE MAKING A DECISION WHETHER OR NOT TO PARTICIPATE. YOUR SIGNATURE INDICATES THAT YOU HAVE DECIDED TO PARTICIPATE HAVING READ THE INFORMATION PROVIDED ABOVE.

_____   _____
Signature of participant   Date

_____   _____
Signature of interviewer   Date

Endnotes

Chapter 1: Who Is Black? Flux and Change in American Racial Identity

1. Although a compromise was adopted allowing respondents to check all racial categories that apply, for civil rights monitoring and enforcement, the data are collapsed back into the previously established five-category system with the addition of the four most common double-race combinations. See Jacob Lew, "Guidance on Aggregation and Allocation of Data on Race for Use in Civil Rights Monitoring and Enforcement," *OMB Bulletin* No. 00-02, 2000.

2. For statistical data on interracial marriages, see Bureau of the Census, *Statistical Abstract of the United States* (Washington, D.C.: Government Printing Office, 1998), Table 67. See also David Harris and Hiromi Ono, "Estimating the Extent of Intimate Contact Between the Races: The Role of Metropolitan Area Factors and Union Type in Mate Selection" (paper presented at the Meetings of the Population Association of America, Los Angeles, 2000), and Susan Kalish, "Interracial Baby Boomlet in Progress?" *Population Today* 20 (1992): 1-2, 9.

3. This description of the multiracial movement is meant to provide an overview of the main arguments presented in favor of adding a multiracial category to the 2000 census. It is admittedly general, and readers interested in a thorough analysis of the multiracial movement should see Heather Dalmage, *The Politics of Multiracialism* (Albany: State University of New York Press, forthcoming).

4. Joel Perlmann, " 'Multiracials', Racial Classification, and American Intermarriage: The Public's Interest" (Working Paper No. 195, The Jerome Levy Economics Institute of Bard College, 1997).

5. Michael Omi and Harold Winant, *Racial Formation in the United States: From the 1960s to the 1990s*, 2d ed. (New York: Routledge & Kegan Paul, 1994).

6. Yehudi Webster, "Twenty-one Arguments for Abolishing Racial Classification," *The Abolitionist Examiner* (www.multiracial.com/abolitionist/word/webster2.html, 2000).

7. Margo Anderson, *The American Census: A Social History* (New Haven, Conn.: Yale University Press, 1990). See also Melissa Nobles, *Shades of Citizen-*

ship: Race and the Census in Modern Politics (Stanford, Calif.: Stanford University Press, 2000).

8. Joel Williamson, *New People: Miscegenation and Mulattos in the United States* (New York: Free Press, 1980).

9. Edward Reuter, *The American Race Problem* (New York: Thomas V. Crowell Co., 1970).

10. Ira Berlin, *Slaves Without Masters: The Free Negro in the Antebellum South* (New York: Pantheon, 1975).

11. John Blassingame, *The Slave Community: Plantation Life in the Antebellum South* (New York: Oxford University Press, 1972).

12. Virginia Dominguez, *White by Definition: Social Classification in Creole Louisiana* (New Brunswick, N.J.: Rutgers University Press, 1986).

13. F. James Davis, *Who Is Black? One Nation's Definition* (University Park: Pennsylvania State University Press, 1991).

14. Ibid.

15. Blassingame, *The Slave Community.*

16. Davis, *Who Is Black?*

17. Ibid.

18. Berlin, *Slaves Without Masters*; Winthrop Jordan, *White Over Black* (Chapel Hill: University of North Carolina Press, 1968); Reuter, *The American Race Problem*; and Williamson, *New People.*

19. Williamson, *New People.*

20. Davis, *Who Is Black?*

21. Williamson, *New People.*

22. Davis, *Who Is Black?*

23. Charles Mangum, *The Legal Status of the Negro in the United States* (Chapel Hill: University of North Carolina Press, 1940).

24. Williamson, *New People.*

25. Cary Wintz, *Black Culture and the Harlem Renaissance* (Houston: Rice University Press, 1988).

26. Davis, *Who Is Black?* Williamson, *New People.*

27. Davis, *Who Is Black?*

28. Ibid.

29. Ibid.

30. Williamson, *New People.*

31. Geneva Smitherman, *Black Talk: Words and Phrases From the Hood to the Amen Corner* (Boston: Houghton Mifflin, 1994), 242.

32. Randall Bland, *Private Pressure on Public Law: The Legal Career of Justice Thurgood Marshall* (Port Washington, N.Y.: Kennikat Press, 1973).

33. Mark Hill, "Color Differences in the Socioeconomic Status of African American Men: Results of a Longitudinal Study," *Social Forces* 78 (2000): 1437-60; Michael Hughes and Bradley Hertel, "The Significance of Color Remains: A Study of Life Chances, Mate Selection, and Ethnic Consciousness Among Black Americans," *Social Forces* 68 (1990): 1105-20; Verna Keith and Cedric Herring, "Skin Tone and Stratification in the Black Community," *American Journal of Sociology* 97 (1991): 760-78; Richard Seltzer and Robert C. Smith, "Color Differences in the Afro-American Community and the Differences They Make," *Journal of Black Studies* 21 (1991): 279-85.

34. Hill, "Color Differences."

35. Robert Margo, *Race and Schooling in the South, 1880-1950* (Chicago: University of Chicago Press, 1990); Hill, "Color Differences."

36. E. Franklin Frazier, *Black Bourgeoisie* (New York: Free Press, 1957). See also Lawrence Otis Graham, *Our Kind of People: Inside America's Black Upper Class* (New York: HarperPerennial, 2000).

37. For examples of what we term early research, see Howard Freeman, David Armor, J. Michael Ross, and Thomas J. Pettigrew, "Color Gradation and Attitudes Among Middle Income Negroes," *American Sociological Review* 31 (1966): 365-74; Norval Glenn, "Negro Prestige Criteria: A Case Study in the Bases of Prestige," *American Journal of Sociology* 68 (1963): 645-57; Gunnar Myrdal, *An American Dilemma: The Negro Problem and Modern Democracy* (New York: Transaction Publishers, 1944); Edward Ransford, "Skin Color, Life Chances and Anti-White Attitudes," *Social Problems* 18 (1970): 164-78. For more contemporary analysis, see Hill, "Color Differences"; Hughes and Hertel, "The Significance of Color Remains"; Keith and Herring, "Skin Tone and Stratification"; and Seltzer and Smith, "Color Differences."

38. Abby Ferber, *White Man Falling: Race, Gender, and White Supremacy* (Lanham, Md.: Rowman and Littlefield, 1998).

39. Robert Park, *Race and Culture* (New York: Free Press, 1950).

40. Michael Hechter, "Group Formation and the Cultural Division of Labor," *American Journal of Sociology* 84 (1978): 293-318.

41. Milton Gordon, *Assimilation in American Life: The Role of Race, Religion, and National Origin* (Oxford, U.K.: Oxford University Press, 1964).

42. Davis, *Who Is Black?*

43. Lewis Killian, *The Impossible Revolution, Phase II: Black Power and the American Dream*, 2d ed. (New York: Random House, 1975).

44. Gordon, *Assimilation in American Life.*

45. For recent research documenting that the multiracial movement was largely run by white, middle-class, suburban mothers of biracial children, see Kim Williams, "Challenging Race as We Know It? The Political Location of the

Multiracial Movement," in *The Politics of Multiracialism: Transforming, Transcending and Challenging Racial Thinking*, ed. Heather Dalmage (Albany: State University of New York Press, forthcoming).

46. Molefi Kete Asante, "Racing to Leave the Race: Black Postmodernists Off-Track," *Black Scholar* 23 (Spring/Fall 1993), 50-51. Reprinted with permission.

47. See, for example, Lisa Jones, *Bulletproof Diva: Tales of Race, Sex, and Hair* (New York: Doubleday, 1994); James McBride, *The Color of Water: A Black Man's Tribute to His White Mother* (New York: Riverhead Books, 1996); Judy Scales-Trent, *Notes of a White Black Woman* (University Park: Pennsylvania State University Press, 1995); and Gregory Williams, *Life on the Color Line: The True Story of a White Boy Who Discovered He Was Black* (New York: Dutton, 1995).

Chapter 2: Biracial Identity Research: Past and Present

1. William Cross, *Shades of Black: Diversity in African American Identity* (Philadelphia: Temple University Press, 1991).

2. Maria Root, "Back to the Drawing Board: Methodological Issues in Research on Multiracial People," in *Racially Mixed People in America*, ed. Maria Root (Newbury Park, Calif.: Sage, 1992); Maria Root, "The Multiracial Experience: Racial Borders as Significant Frontier in Race Relations," in *The Multiracial Experience: Racial Borders as the New Frontier*, ed. Maria Root (Thousand Oaks, Calif.: Sage, 1996).

3. Christine Kerwin, Joseph Ponterotto, Barbara Jackson, and Abigail Harris, "Racial Identity in Biracial Children: A Qualitative Investigation," *Journal of Counseling Psychology* 40 (1993): 221-31; Kerry Ann Rockquemore, "Between Black and White: Exploring the Biracial Experience," *Race and Society* 1 (1999): 197-212.

4. Erik Erikson, *Identity: Youth and Crisis* (New York: W. W. Norton, 1968).

5. Ibid., 328.

6. For black identity models, see Cross, *Shades of Black*. For a model specific to biracial identity development, see W. Carlos Poston, "The Biracial Identity Development Model: A Needed Addition," *Journal of Counseling and Development* 69 (1990): 152-55.

7. Roger Herring, "Developing Biracial Ethnic Identity: A Review of the Increasing Dilemma," *Journal of Multicultural Counseling and Development* 23 (1995): 29-38; Jewelle Taylor Gibbs, "Biracial Adolescents," in *Children of Color: Psychological Interventions With Culturally Diverse Youth*, ed. Jewelle Taylor Gibbs and Larke-Nahme Huang (New York: Jossey-Bass, 1997).

8. Gibbs, "Biracial Adolescents," 332.

9. Herbert Blumer, *Symbolic Interactionism: Perspective and Method* (Englewood Cliffs, N.J.: Prentice Hall, 1969).

10. Gregory Stone, "Appearance and the Self," in *Human Behavior and Social Processes,* ed. A. M. Rose (Boston: Houghton Mifflin, 1962).

11. Jean Phinney, "Ethnic Identity in Adolescents and Adults: Review of Research," *Psychological Bulletin* 108 (1990): 499-514.

12. See William Cross, "The Negro-to-Black Conversion Experience: Toward a Psychology of Black Liberation," *Black World* 20 (1971): 13-27; Cross, *Shades of Black.*

13. Lynda Field, "Piecing Together the Puzzle: Self-Concept and Group Identity in Biracial Black/White Youth," in *The Multiracial Experience,* ed. Maria Root (Newbury Park, Calif.: Sage, 1996), 216.

14. Field, "Piecing Together the Puzzle"; Ana Mari Cauce, Yumi Hiraga, Craig Mason, Tanya Aguilar, Nydia Ordonez, and Nancy Gonzales, "Between a Rock and a Hard Place: Social Adjustment of Biracial Youth," in *Racially Mixed People in America,* ed. Maria Root (Newbury Park, Calif.: Sage, 1992); Jewelle Taylor Gibbs and Alice Hines, "Negotiating Ethnic Identity: Issues for Black-White Biracial Adolescents," in *Racially Mixed People in America,* ed. Maria Root (Newbury Park, Calif.: Sage, 1992).

15. Kathlyn Gay, *The Rainbow Effect: Interracial Families* (New York: Franklin Watts, 1987); R. Johnson and C. Nagoshi, "The Adjustment of Offspring Within Group and Interracial/Intercultural Marriages: A Comparison of Personality Factor Scores," *Journal of Marriage and the Family* 48 (1986): 279-84; Alvin Poussaint, "Study of Interracial Children Presents Positive Picture," *Interracial Books for Children* 15 (1984): 9-10.

16. M. Lyles, A. Yancey, C. Grace, and J. Carter, "Racial Identity and Self-Esteem: Problems Peculiar to Bi-Racial Children," *Journal of the American Academy of Child Psychiatry* 24 (1985): 150-53; D. Sebring, "Considerations in Counseling Interracial Children," *Journal of Non-White Concerns in Personnel and Guidance* 13 (1985): 3-9.

17. Fernando Henriques, *Children of Conflict: A Study of Interracial Sex and Marriage* (New York: Dutton, 1974); Joyce Ladner, *Mixed Families* (New York: Anchor Press, 1977); Vladimir Piskacek and Marlene Golub, "Children of Interracial Marriage," in *Interracial Marriage: Expectations and Reality,* ed. Irving Stuart and Lawrence Abt (New York: Grossman, 1973).

18. Cauce et al., "Between a Rock and a Hard Place"; Field, "Piecing Together the Puzzle." See also W. Gunthorpe, "Skin Color Recognition, Preference, and Identification in Interracial Children: A Comparative Study," *Dissertation Abstracts International,* 38 (1978): 3468.

19. Piskacek and Golub, "Children of Interracial Marriage." See also V. Sommers, "The Impact of Dual Cultural Membership on Identity," *Psychiatry* 27 (1964): 332-44.

20. Douglas Besharov and Timothy Sullivan, "One Flesh," *The New Democrat* 8 (1996): 19-21.

21. Roger Herring, "Biracial Children: An Increasing Concern for Elementary and Middle School Counselors," *Elementary School Guidance and Counseling* 27 (1992): 123-30. The quoted material is from Gibbs, "Biracial Adolescents," 332-33.

22. J. Faulkner and G. Kich, "Assessment and Engagement Stages in Therapy with the Interracial Family," *Family Therapy Collections* 6 (1983): 78-90; Jewelle Taylor Gibbs, "Black Students/White Universities: Different Expectations," *Personnel and Guidance Journal* 51 (1973): 463-69; Lyles et al., "Racial Identity and Self-Esteem"; Sebring, "Considerations in Counseling Interracial Children."

23. Field, "Piecing Together the Puzzle."

24. See Poussaint, "Study of Interracial Children"; and E. Porterfield, *Black and White Marriages: An Ethnographic Study of Black-White Families* (Chicago: Nelson-Hall, 1978).

25. Theresa Williams, "Race as Process: Reassessing the 'What Are You?' Encounters of Biracial Individuals," in *The Multiracial Experience*, ed. Maria Root (Thousand Oaks, Calif.: Sage, 1996).

26. Omi and Winant, *Racial Formation in the United States*, 62.

27. Dorcas Bowles, "Bi-racial Identity: Children Born to African-American and White Couples," *Clinical Social Work Journal* 21 (1993): 417-28.

28. Herring, "Biracial Children"; Gibbs, "Biracial Adolescents."

29. Rockquemore, "Between Black and White."

30. See Rockquemore, "Between Black and White," and Kathleen Odell Korgen, *From Black to Biracial* (New York: Praeger, 1998).

31. Bowles, "Bi-racial Identity."

32. Kerwin et al., "Racial Identity in Biracial Children."

33. Herring, "Biracial Children"; Gibbs, "Biracial Adolescents," 334.

34. Kerwin et al., "Racial Identity in Biracial Children."

35. Bowles, "Bi-racial Identity."

36. Gibbs, "Biracial Adolescents"; Herring, "Biracial Children."

37. Sebring, "Considerations in Counseling Interracial Children."

38. Gibbs, "Biracial Adolescents"; Herring, "Biracial Children."

39. Piskacek and Golub, "Children of Interracial Marriage"; Sommers, "The Impact of Dual Cultural Membership"; Paul Adams, "Counseling With Interracial Couples and Their Children in the South," in *Interracial Marriage: Expecta-*

tions and Reality, ed. I. R. Stuart and L. E. Abt (New York: Grossman, 1973); Lyles et al., "Racial Identity and Self-Esteem"; Sebring, "Considerations in Counseling Interracial Children"; S. Benson, *Ambiguous Ethnicity* (London: Cambridge University Press, 1981); Henriques, *Children of Conflict;* Ladner, *Mixed Families;* R. McRoy and E. Freeman, "Racial Identity Issues Among Mixed-Race Children," *Social Work in Education* 8 (1986): 164-74; J. Teicher, "Some Observations on Identity Problems in Children of Negro-White Marriages," *Journal of Nervous and Mental Disease* 146 (1968): 249-56.

40. Poston, "The Biracial Identity Development Model."

41. Herring, "Developing Biracial Ethnic Identity."

42. Names of participating institutions have been replaced by pseudonyms to provide anonymity to those institutions and the students participating in the study.

43. Root, "Back to the Drawing Board"; Steven Taylor and Robert Bogdan, *Introduction to Qualitative Research Methods: The Search for Meanings* (New York: John Wiley, 1984).

44. Catherine Marshall and Gretchen Rossman, *Designing Qualitative Research* (Newbury Park, Calif.: Sage, 1989).

45. Root, "The Multiracial Experience."

46. For a description of the data analysis procedure we followed, see G. McCracken, *The Long Interview,* Sage University Paper Series on Qualitative Research Methods, Vol. 13 (Newbury Park, Calif.: Sage, 1988). This procedure includes the following five stages: (a) initially sorting the important from the unimportant data, (b) examining the data for logical relationships and/or contradictions, (c) rereading the initial transcripts to confirm or disconfirm the relationships that are emerging, (d) identifying general themes and sorting them in hierarchical fashion, and (e) reviewing the emergent themes in each interview and determining how they can be synthesized. We began with a transcription of the audiotaped interviews, which we then read and reread to form categories related to the research question. The important pieces of data were "cut and pasted" to form a second transcript, which was read and reread to question, reconfigure, and finally confirm categories of responses. From this point, major and minor categories were determined to construct a descriptive map of the various ways in which the respondents understood their racial identity.

47. Specifically, the survey received administrative approval at Metro Community College and approval of the Institutional Review Board for the Protection of Human Subjects at Urban University and Catholic University.

48. Overall, we consider the final sample size satisfactory given that researchers using the Adolescent Health data set, a nationally representative random sample of 83,135 adolescents, has found that only 108 of the total cases are

black/white biracials. See David Harris, "An Empirical Look at the Social Construction of Race: The Case of Mixed-Race Adolescents" (paper presented at the annual meeting of the American Sociological Association, Washington, D.C., August, 2000).

49. See Root, "Back to the Drawing Board," for a thorough discussion of unique methodological issues faced by researchers studying the biracial population.

Chapter 3: What Does Biracial Identity Mean?

1. Perlmann, "Multiracials."

2. Blumer, *Symbolic Interactionism.*

3. Stone, "Appearance and the Self."

4. Andrew Weigert, "The Substantival Self: A Primitive Term for a Sociological Psychology," *Philosophy of the Social Sciences* 5 (1975): 43-62.

5. All names are pseudonyms.

6. Gloria Anzaldua, *Borderlands/La Frontera: The New Mestiza* (San Francisco: Spinsters/Aunt Lute Foundation, 1987).

7. Bowles, "Bi-racial Identity"; Philip Brown, "Biracial Identity and Social Marginality," *Child and Adolescent Social Work Journal* 7 (1990): 319-37; G. Reginald Daniel, "Black and White Identity in the New Millennium: Unsevering the Ties That Bind," in *The Multiracial Experience: Racial Borders as the New Frontier,* ed. Maria Root (Thousand Oaks, Calif.: Sage, 1996); Field, "Piecing Together the Puzzle"; Christine Hall, "The Ethnic Identity of Racially Mixed People: A Study of Black-Japanese" (Ph.D. diss., University of California, Los Angeles, 1980); Herring, "Developing Biracial Ethnic Identity"; Poston, "The Biracial Identity Development Model"; and Gibbs, "Biracial Adolescents."

8. Herring, "Developing Biracial Ethnic Identity"; Deborah Johnson, "Developmental Pathways: Toward an Ecological Theoretical Formulation of Race Identity in Black-White Biracial Children," in *Racially Mixed People in America,* ed. Maria Root (Newbury Park, Calif.: Sage, 1992); Kerwin et al., "Racial Identity in Biracial Children"; George Kich, "The Developmental Process of Asserting a Biracial, Bicultural Identity," in *Racially Mixed People in America,* ed. Maria Root (Newbury Park, Calif.: Sage, 1992); Poston, "The Biracial Identity Development Model"; Francis Wardle, "Are We Sensitive to Interracial Children's Special Identity Needs?" *Young Children* 43 (1987): 53-59; and Francis Wardle, *Biracial Identity: An Ecological and Developmental Model* (Denver, CO: Center for the Study of Biracial Children, 1992).

9. Hall, *The Ethnic Identity of Racially Mixed People.*

10. Barbara Tizard and Ann Phoenix, "The Identity of Mixed Parentage Adolescents," *Journal of Child Psychology and Psychiatry* 36 (1995): 1399-1410.

11. Daniel, "Black and White Identity," 133.

12. Carla Bradshaw, "Beauty and the Beast: On Racial Ambiguity," in *Racially Mixed People in America*, ed. Maria Root (Newbury Park, Calif.: Sage, 1992); Field, "Piecing Together the Puzzle"; Rebecca King and Kimberly DaCosta, "Changing Face, Changing Race: The Remaking of Race in the Japanese American and African American Communities," in *The Multiracial Experience*, ed. Maria Root (Thousand Oaks, Calif.: Sage, 1996); Williams, "Race as Process."

13. Herring, "Developing Biracial Ethnic Identity"; Johnson, "Developmental Pathways"; Kerwin et al., "Racial Identity in Biracial Children"; Kich, "The Developmental Process"; Poston, "The Biracial Identity Development Model"; Wardle, "Are We Sensitive?"; Wardle, *Biracial Identity.*

14. All interviews presented in this chapter were conducted by Kerry Ann Rockquemore. The vignettes are taken from interviewer notes, hence the use of *I* as opposed to *we.*

15. Maria Root, "Resolving 'Other' Status: Identity Development of Biracial Individuals," *Women and Therapy* 9 (1990): 185-205; Root, "The Multiracial Experience."

16. Root, "Resolving 'Other' Status," 588.

17. Robert Lifton, *The Protean Self: Human Resilience in an Age of Fragmentation* (New York: Basic Books, 1993).

18. Daniel, "Black and White Identity"; Robin Miller, "The Human Ecology of Multiracial Identity," in *Racially Mixed People in America*, ed. Maria Root (Newbury Park, Calif.: Sage, 1992); Root, "Resolving 'Other' Status"; Tizard and Phoenix, "The Identity of Mixed Parentage Adolescents."

19. Root, "Resolving 'Other' Status."

20. Ibid., xxi.

21. Cookie Stephan, "Mixed-Heritage Individuals: Ethnic Identity and Trait Characteristics," in *Racially Mixed People in America*, ed. Maria Root (Newbury Park, Calif.: Sage, 1992); Root, "Resolving 'Other' Status."

22. Daniel, "Black and White Identity."

23. Tizard and Phoenix, "The Identity of Mixed Parentage Adolescents."

24. Miller, "The Human Ecology of Multiracial Identity."

25. Daniel, "Black and White Identity."

26. Park, *Race and Culture.*

27. The total percentage of our respondents falling into each of the four identity types does not total 100 percent because we provided individuals with the option of writing in their own response to our survey question on racial identity. Only 8 percent of respondents chose to write in something other than what was provided. Many of the write-in responses were subtle variations of the options we provided and could have been collapsed back into the categories presented in this chapter. However, we chose not to do this and treated these cases as missing data. The fact that 92 percent of our sample found the range of responses we provided accurately described their racial identity lends support to the authenticity of our multidimensional model of racial identity among biracial people.

28. Bradshaw, "Beauty and the Beast"; Field, "Piecing Together the Puzzle"; King and DaCosta, "Changing Face, Changing Race"; and Williams, "Race as Process."

Chapter 4: Socialization and Biracial Identity

1. Richard Allen, Michael Dawson, and Ronald Brown, "A Schema-Based Approach to Modeling an African-American Racial Belief System," *American Political Science Review* 83 (1989): 421-41; Clifford Broman, Harold Neighbors, and James Jackson, "Racial Group Identification Among Black Adults," *Social Forces* 67 (1988): 146-58; David Demo and Michael Hughes, "Socialization and Racial Identity Among Black Americans," *Social Psychology Quarterly* 53 (1990): 364-74; Mary Waters, *Ethnic Options: Choosing Identities in America* (Berkeley: University of California Press, 1990).

2. Waters, *Ethnic Options*.

3. Peter Burke, "The Self: Measurement Requirements from an Interactionist Perspective," *Social Psychology Quarterly* 43 (1980): 18-29; quotation is on page 18.

4. Ethnic identity in this context refers to individuals several generations removed from the immigration experience. For analysis of the multidimensional nature of racial identity, see Broman, Neighbors, and Jackson, "Racial Group Identification"; and Patricia Gurin, Arthur H. Miller, and Gerald Gurin, "Stratum Identification and Consciousness," *Social Psychology Quarterly* 43, (1980): 30-47.

5. Broman, Neighbors, and Jackson, "Racial Group Identification," 148.

6. Allen, Dawson, and Brown, "A Schema-Based Approach"; William Cross, "Black Identity: Rediscovering the Distinction Between Personal Identity and Reference Group Orientation," in *Beginnings: The Social and Affective*

Development of Black Children, ed. Margaret Spencer, Geraldine Brookins, and Walter Allen (Hillsdale, N.J.: Lawrence Erlbaum, 1985); Demo and Hughes, "Socialization and Racial Identity."

7. Broman, Neighbors, and Jackson, "Racial Group Identification"; Allen, Dawson, and Brown, "A Schema-Based Approach"; and Demo and Hughes, "Socialization and Racial Identity."

8. A multidimensional black identity may be composed of various dimensions, including group evaluation (positive or negative), closeness to other members of the group (high or low), and group autonomy (high or low preference).

9. Erving Goffman, *The Presentation of Self in Everyday Life* (New York: Anchor Doubleday, 1959).

10. Stone, "Appearance and the Self."

11. Field, "Piecing Together the Puzzle"; Tizard and Phoenix, "The Identity of Mixed Parentage Adolescents."

12. Brown, "Biracial Identity and Social Marginality."

13. Skin color was measured using Item 17 in the survey, whereas appearance was measured using Item 97. See Appendix F for further details.

14. Root, "Resolving 'Other' Status"; Rockquemore, "Between Black and White"; Williams, "Race as Process."

15. For an excellent review of the literature in the field of psychology, see Phinney, "Ethnic Identity."

16. When asked which of the following best describes their physical appearance, using responses that have the assumptions that *other people* make about themselves, we see that the most common (56.2 percent) response was that "My physical features are ambiguous, most people assume that I am black." Yet, there is variation here, with 17.2 percent responding that "I look black and most people assume that I am black," 16.6 percent stating that their features "are ambiguous, people do not assume I am black," and 10.1 percent responding that "I physically look white, I could *pass.*"

17. Bowles, "Bi-racial Identity"; Herring, "Biracial Children": 123-30; Gibbs, "Black Students/White Universities"; Poussaint, "Study of Interracial Children."

18. Root, "Back to the Drawing Board," 6.

19. Hall, "The Ethnic Identity of Racially Mixed People"; C. P. Porter, "Social Reasons for Skin Tone Preferences of Black School-Aged Children," *American Journal of Orthopsychiatry* 61 (1991): 149-54; Rockquemore, "Between Black and White"; Root, "Resolving 'Other' Status."

20. F. James Davis, *Minority-Dominant Relations* (Arlington Heights, Ill.: AHM Publishing Co., 1978). See also Jon Michael Spencer, *The New Colored*

People: The Mixed-Race Movement in America (New York: New York University Press, 1997).

21. Rockquemore, "Between Black and White."

22. Rockquemore, "Between Black and White"; A. Wade Boykin and Forrest D. Toms, "Black Child Socialization: A Conceptual Framework," in *Black Children: Social, Educational, and Parental Environments,* ed. Harriette P. McAdoo and John Lewis McAdoo (Beverly Hills, Calif.: Sage, 1985); R. Miller and B. Miller, "Mothering the Biracial Child: Bridging the Gaps between African-American and White Parenting Styles," *Women and Therapy* 10 (1990): 169-80; Brown, "Biracial Identity and Social Marginality."

23. Miller and Miller "Mothering the Biracial Child"; Rockquemore, "Between Black and White."

24. Field, "Piecing Together the Puzzle."

25. Viktor Gecas, "Contexts of Socialization," in *Social Psychology: Sociological Perspectives,* ed. Morris Rosenberg and Ralph Turner (New York: Basic Books, 1981).

26. David Demo, Stephen Small, and Ritch Savin-Williams, "Family Relations and the Self-Esteem of Adolescents and Their Parents," *Journal of Marriage and the Family* 49 (1987): 705-15; Viktor Gecas and Michael Schwalbe, "Parental Behavior and Dimensions of Adolescent Self-Evaluation," *Journal of Marriage and the Family* 48 (1986): 37-46.

27. Demo and Hughes, "Socialization and Racial Identity."

28. For work on racial socialization, see Boykin and Toms, "Black Child Socialization." Herring, "Biracial Children," describes difficulties in socialization among biracials.

29. Morris Rosenberg, "The Dissonant Context and the Adolescent Self-Concept," in *Adolescence in the Life Cycle,* ed. Sigmund Dragastin and Glen Elder (New York: Wiley, 1975); Morris Rosenberg, *Conceiving the Self* (New York: Basic Books, 1979).

30. William McGuire, Claire McGuire, P. Child, and T. Fujioka, "Salience of Ethnicity in the Spontaneous Self-Concept as a Function of One's Ethnic Distinctiveness in the Social Environment," *Journal of Personality and Social Psychology* 36 (1978): 511-20.

31. Viktor Gecas, "The Influence of Social Class on Socialization," in *Contemporary Theories About the Family,* ed. Wesley R. Burr, Reuben Hill, F. Ivan Nye, and Ira L. Reiss (New York: Free Press, 1979).

32. Demo and Hughes, "Socialization and Racial Identity."

33. Ibid.

34. John Clausen, *The Life Course: A Sociological Perspective* (Englewood Cliffs, N.J.: Prentice Hall, 1986); Glen Elder, "History and the Life Course," in

Biography and Society, ed. Daniel Bertaux (Beverly Hills, Calif.: Sage, 1981); and Viktor Gecas and Jeylan Mortimer, "Stability and Change in the Self-Concept From Adolescence to Adulthood," in *Self and Identity: Individual Change and Development,* ed. Terry Honess and Krysia Yardley (New York: Routledge & Kegan Paul, 1987).

35. Jerry Suls and Brian Mullen, "From the Cradle to the Grave: Comparison and Self-Evaluation Across the Life-Span," in *Psychological Perspectives on the Self,* ed. Jerry Suls (Hillsdale, N.J.: Lawrence Erlbaum, 1982); Michael Basseches, *Dialectical Reasoning and Adult Development,* (Norwood, N.J.: Ablex, 1984); J. L. Horn and G. Donaldson, "Cognitive Development in Adulthood," in *Constancy and Change in Human Development,* ed. Orville Brim and Jerome Kagan (Cambridge, Mass.: Harvard University Press, 1980); K. Schaie, "The Seattle Longitudinal Study: A 21-Year Exploration of Psychometric Intelligence in Adulthood," in *Longitudinal Studies of Adult Psychological Development,* ed. K. Schaie (New York: Guilford, 1983).

36. Demo, Small, and Savin-Williams, "Family Relations."

37. Michael Hughes and David Demo, "Self-Perceptions of Black Americans: Self-Esteem and Personal Efficacy," *American Journal of Sociology* 95 (1989): 132-59; Suzanne Ortega, Robert Crutchfield, and William Rushing, "Race Differences in Elderly Personal Well-Being," *Research on Aging* 5 (1983): 101-18.

38. Allen, Dawson, and Brown, "A Schema-Based Approach"; Broman, Neighbors, and Jackson, "Racial Group Identification."

39. Morris Rosenberg and Roberta Simmons, *Black and White Self-Esteem: The Urban School Child* (Washington, D.C.: American Sociological Association, 1972); Rosenberg, *Conceiving the Self;* Broman, Neighbors, and Jackson, "Racial Group Identification."

40. Hall, "The Ethnic Identity of Racially Mixed People"; Field, "Piecing Together the Puzzle."

41. Waters, *Ethnic Options.*

Chapter 5: The Color Complex: Appearance and Biracial Identity

1. Daniel, "Black and White Identity"; Rockquemore, "Between Black and White"; Root, "Back to the Drawing Board"; Root, "The Multiracial Experience"; Kathy Russell, Midge Wilson, and Ronald Hall, *The Color Complex: The Politics of Skin Color Among African Americans* (New York: Anchor, 1992); Werner Sollors, *Neither Black Nor White Yet Both* (Oxford, U.K.: Oxford University Press, 1997).

2. Davis, *Who Is Black?*; Spencer, *The New Colored People*; Yehudi Webster, *Against the Multicultural Agenda: A Critical Thinking Alternative* (Westport, Conn.: Greenwood, 1997).

3. Omi and Winant, *Racial Formation in the United States.*

4. Goffman, *The Presentation of Self.*

5. Gustav Ichheiser, *Appearances and Realities: Misunderstanding in Human Relations* (San Francisco: Jossey-Bass, 1970).

6. Stone, "Appearance and the Self."

7. Nancy Boyd-Franklin, *Black Families in Therapy: A Multisystems Approach* (New York: Guilford, 1989); Aminifu Harvey, "The Issue of Skin Color in Psychotherapy With African Americans," *Families in Society: The Journal of Contemporary Human Services* 76 (1995): 3-10; Hughes and Hertel, "The Significance of Color Remains"; A. M. Neal and M. L. Wilson, "The Role of Skin Color and Feature in the Black Community: Implications for Black Women and Therapy," *Clinical Psychology Review* 9 (1989): 323-33; Porter, "Social Reasons"; Judith Porter and Robert Washington, "Minority identity and Self-Esteem," *Annual Review of Sociology* 19 (1993): 139-61.

8. Keith and Herring, "Skin Tone and Stratification."

9. Bowles, "Bi-racial Identity"; Brown, "Biracial Identity and Social Marginality"; Daniel, "Black and White Identity"; Field, "Piecing Together the Puzzle"; Hall, "The Ethnic Identity of Racially Mixed People"; Tizard and Phoenix, "The Identity of Mixed Parentage Adolescents."

10. Brown, "Biracial Identity and Social Marginality."

11. Daniel, "Black and White Identity."

12. Bowles, "Bi-racial Identity."

13. Tizard and Phoenix, "The Identity of Mixed Parentage Adolescents."

14. Russell, Wilson, and Hall, *The Color Complex.*

15. David Brunsma and Kerry Ann Rockquemore, "Negotiations on the Color Line: Phenotype, Appearances, and (Bi)racial Identity," *Identity* 3 (2001).

16. Root, "Resolving 'Other' Status"; Rockquemore, "Between Black and White."

17. Stone, "Appearance and the Self."

18. Ibid.

19. Ibid., 188-89.

20. Stone, "Appearance and the Self." See also Candace West and Don H. Zimmerman, "Doing Gender," *Gender and Society* 1 (1987): 125-51.

21. Stone, "Appearance and the Self," 103.

22. Charles Horton Cooley, *Human Nature and the Social Order* (New York: Scribner's, 1902).

23. George Herbert Mead, *Mind, Self, and Society* (Chicago: University of Chicago Press, 1934).

24. Cooley, *Human Nature and the Social Order.*

25. Ibid.

26. Mead, *Mind, Self, and Society*; Cooley, *Human Nature and the Social Order.*

27. Stone, "Appearance and the Self," 193.

28. Ibid., 194.

29. Anselm Strauss, *Mirrors and Masks: The Search for Identity* (Glencoe, IL: Free Press, 1959).

30. Weigert, "The Substantival Self," 47.

31. Goffman, *The Presentation of Self.*

32. Item 18 in Survey of Biracial Experiences (Appendix F).

33. The survey items measuring the racial composition of respondents' social networks (Items 19 through 29 in Survey of Biracial Experiences, Appendix F) indicated the level of interracial contact over their lifetime. This measure is a modification of the interracial contact variable used by Demo and Hughes, "Socialization and Racial Identity." Individuals were asked to assess the racial composition of their (a) grammar and elementary school, (b) closest friends in elementary school, (c) junior high school, (d) high school, (e) closest friends in high school, (f) college, (g) neighborhood while growing up, (h) present neighborhood, (i) closest friends today, (j) church or place of worship usually attended, and (k) present workplace, if employed. The responses were coded in the following way: 0 = *All whites,* 1 = *Mostly whites,* 2 = *About half black,* 3 = *Mostly blacks,* 4 = *All blacks.* From these items, we constructed two scales of social network composition: (a) a pre-adult scale (Items 1 through 5, and 7) and an adult scale (Items 6 and 8 through 11). Each scale was computed by summing across the items: pre-adult scale (α = .93), adult scale (α = .78).

34. Items 64 and 65 in Survey of Biracial Experiences (Appendix F).

35. Root, "Back to the Drawing Board."

36. Russell, Wilson, and Hall, *The Color Complex,* 63.

37. Readers interested in details of the specific quantitative analyses discussed here should see Brunsma and Rockquemore, "Negotiations on the Color Line."

38. Williams, "Race as Process."

39. Although John's racial identity as white withstood the revelation that his biological father was black, it would be interesting to see how, or if, his identity may change when (or if) he becomes a father himself. It is one thing to learn that his own biological father, whom he has never met nor will ever meet, was black. It would be quite another for John to have a child with a black appearance.

It is precisely these types of questions that necessitate the addition of longitudinal analysis to research on biracial identity.

40. Claud Anderson and Rue Cromwell, " 'Black Is Beautiful' and the Color Preferences of Afro-American Youth," *Journal of Negro Education* 46 (1977): 76-88; Ronald Hall, "Bias Among African Americans Regarding Skin Color: Implications for Social Work Practice," *Research on Social Work Practice* 2 (1992): 479-86; Tracy L. Robinson and Janie V. Ward, "African American Adolescents and Skin Color," *Journal of Black Psychology* 21 (1995): 256-74; Russell, Wilson, and Hall, *The Color Complex.*

Chapter 6: Who Is Black Today, and Who Will Be Black Tomorrow?

1. Williams, "Challenging Race."

2. Spencer, *The New Colored People,* 4.

3. Davis, *Who Is Black?*

4. Ibid.

5. Spencer, *The New Colored People.*

6. Davis, *Who Is Black?*

7. Ibid., 180.

8. Jennifer Hochschild, *Facing Up to the American Dream: Race, Class, and the Soul of the Nation* (Princeton, N.J.: Princeton University Press, 1996).

9. See Heather Dalmage, *Tripping on the Color Line: Black-White Multiracial Families in a Racially Divided World* (New Brunswick, N.J.: Rutgers University Press, 2000).

10. Spencer, *The New Colored People,* 73.

11. Davis, *Who Is Black?*

12. Ibid.

13. Myrdal, *An American Dilemma,* 113.

14. Davis, *Who Is Black?,* 186.

15. Halford Fairchild, "Scientific Racism: The Cloak of Objectivity," *Journal of Social Issues,* 47 (1991): 101-15; quotation on page 103.

16. Dalmage, *Tripping on the Color Line,* 13.

17. Appiah was quoted in Lawrence Wright, "One Drop of Blood," *The New Yorker* (July 24, 1994), 46.

18. The first quote is taken from a personal correspondence written by Newt Gingrich to the Director of the Office of Management and Budget, July 1, 1997

(available online at http://www.projectrace.com/hot_news.html). The second quote is from Jerelyn Eddings, "Counting a 'New' Type of American: The Dicey Politics of Creating a 'Multiracial' Category in the Census," *U.S. News and World Report* (July 7, 1997), A1.

19. Joe Feagin, and Melvin Sikes, *Living With Racism: The Black Middle-Class Experience* (Boston: Beacon, 1994).

References

Adams, Paul. "Counseling With Interracial Couples and Their Children in the South," in *Interracial Marriage: Expectations and Reality*, edited by I. R. Stuart and L. E. Abt. New York: Grossman, 1973.

Allen, Richard, Michael Dawson, and Ronald Brown. "A Schema-Based Approach to Modeling an African-American Racial Belief System." *American Political Science Review* 83 (1989): 421-41.

Anderson, Claud, and Rue L. Cromwell. " 'Black Is Beautiful' and the Color Preferences of Afro-American Youth." *Journal of Negro Education* 46 (1977): 76-88.

Anderson, Margo. *The American Census: A Social History*. New Haven, Conn.: Yale University Press, 1990.

Anzaldua, Gloria. *Borderlands/La Frontera: The New Mestiza*. San Francisco: Spinsters/ Aunt Lute Foundation, 1987.

Asante, Molefi Kete. "Racing to Leave the Race: Black Postmodernists Off-Track." *Black Scholar* 23, nos. 3-4 (1993): 50-51.

Basseches, Michael. *Dialectical Reasoning and Adult Development*. Norwood, N.J.: Ablex, 1984

Benson, S. *Ambiguous Ethnicity*. London: Cambridge University Press, 1981.

Berlin, Ira. *Slaves Without Masters: The Free Negro in the Antebellum South*. New York: Pantheon, 1975.

Besharov, Douglas, and Timothy Sullivan. "One Flesh." *The New Democrat* 8, no. 4 (1996): 19-21.

Bland, Randall W. *Private Pressure on Public Law: The Legal Career of Justice Thurgood Marshall*. Port Washington, N.Y.: Kennikat Press, 1973.

Blassingame, John W. *The Slave Community: Plantation Life in the Antebellum South*. New York: Oxford University Press, 1972.

Blumer, Herbert. *Symbolic Interactionism: Perspective and Method*. Englewood Cliffs, N.J.: Prentice Hall, 1969.

Bowles, Dorcas D. "Bi-racial Identity: Children Born to African-American and White Couples." *Clinical Social Work Journal* 21, no. 4 (1993): 417-28.

Boyd-Franklin, Nancy. *Black Families in Therapy: A Multisystems Approach*. New York: Guilford, 1989.

Boykin, A. Wade, and Forrest D. Toms. "Black Child Socialization: A Conceptual Framework." In *Black Children: Social, Educational, and Parental Environments,* edited by Harriette P. McAdoo and John Lewis McAdoo. Beverly Hills, Calif.: Sage, 1985.

Bradshaw, Carla. "Beauty and the Beast: On Racial Ambiguity." In *Racially Mixed People in America,* edited by Maria Root. Newbury Park, Calif.: Sage, 1992.

Broman, Clifford, Harold Neighbors, and James Jackson. "Racial Group Identification Among Black Adults." *Social Forces* 67 (1988): 146-58.

Brown, Philip M. "Biracial Identity and Social Marginality." *Child and Adolescent Social Work Journal* 7, no. 4 (1990): 319-37.

Brunsma, David, and Kerry Ann Rockquemore. "Negotiations on the Color Line: Phenotype, Appearances, and (Bi)racial Identity." *Identity* 3, no. 1 (2001).

Burke, Peter. "The Self: Measurement Requirements From an Interactionist Perspective." *Social Psychology Quarterly* 43 (1980): 18-29.

Cauce, Ana Mari, Yumi Hiraga, Craig Mason, Tanya Aguilar, Nydia Ordonez, and Nancy Gonzales. "Between a Rock and a Hard Place: Social Adjustment of Biracial Youth." In *Racially Mixed People in America,* edited by Maria Root. Newbury Park, Calif.: Sage, 1992.

Clausen, John. *The Life Course: A Sociological Perspective.* Englewood Cliffs, N.J.: Prentice Hall, 1986.

Cooley, Charles Horton. *Human Nature and the Social Order.* New York: Scribner's, 1902.

Cross, William. "The Negro-to-Black Conversion Experience: Toward a Psychology of Black liberation." *Black World* 20 (1971): 13-27.

———. "Black Identity: Rediscovering the Distinction Between Personal Identity and Reference Group Orientation." In *Beginnings: The Social and Affective Development of Black Children,* edited by Margaret Spencer, Geraldine Brookins, and Walter Allen. Hillsdale, N.J.: Lawrence Erlbaum, 1985.

———. *Shades of Black: Diversity in African American Identity.* Philadelphia: Temple University Press, 1991.

Dalmage, Heather. *Tripping on the Color Line: Black-White Multiracial Families in a Racially Divided World.* New Brunswick, N.J.: Rutgers University Press, 2000.

———. *The Politics of Multiracialism.* Albany: State University of New York Press, forthcoming.

Daniel, G. Reginald. "Black and White Identity in the New Millennium: Unsevering the Ties That Bind." In *The Multiracial Experience: Racial Borders as the New Frontier,* edited by Maria Root. Thousand Oaks, Calif.: Sage, 1996.

Davis, F. James. *Minority-Dominant Relations.* Arlington Heights, Ill.: AHM Publishing, 1978.

———. *Who Is Black? One Nation's Definition.* University Park: Pennsylvania State University Press, 1991.

Demo, David, and Michael Hughes. "Socialization and Racial Identity Among Black Americans." *Social Psychology Quarterly* 53 (1990): 364-74.

Demo, David, Stephen Small, and Ritch Savin-Williams. "Family Relations and the Self-Esteem of Adolescents and Their Parents." *Journal of Marriage and the Family* 49 (1987): 705-15.

Dominguez, Virginia R. *White by Definition: Social Classification in Creole Louisiana.* New Brunswick, N.J.: Rutgers University Press, 1986.

Eddings, Jerelyn. "Counting a 'New' Type of American: The Dicey Politics of Creating a 'Multiracial' Category in the Census." *U.S. News and World Report,* 7 July 1997.

Elder, Glen. "History and the Life Course." In *Biography and Society,* edited by Daniel Bertaux. Beverly Hills, Calif.: Sage, 1981.

Erikson, Erik H. *Identity: Youth and Crisis.* New York: W. W. Norton, 1968.

Fairchild, Halford. "Scientific Racism: The Cloak of Objectivity." *Journal of Social Issues,* 47, no. 3 (1991): 101-15.

Faulkner, J., and G. Kich. "Assessment and Engagement Stages in Therapy With the Interracial Family." *Family Therapy Collections* 6 (1983): 78-90.

Feagin, Joe, and Melvin Sikes. *Living With Racism: The Black Middle-Class Experience.* Boston: Beacon, 1994.

Ferber, Abby. *White Man Falling: Race, Gender, and White Supremacy.* Lanham Md.: Rowman and Littlefield, 1998.

Fields, Lynda. "Piecing Together the Puzzle: Self-Concept and Group Identity in Biracial People in America l Black/White Youth." In *The Multiracial Experience,* edited by Maria Root. Thousand Oaks, Calif.: Sage, 1996.

Frazier, E. Franklin. *Black Bourgeoisie.* New York: Free Press, 1957.

Freeman, Howard E., David Armor, J. Michael Ross, and Thomas J. Pettigrew. "Color Gradation and Attitudes Among Middle Income Negroes." *American Sociological Review* 31 (1966): 365-74.

Gay, Kathlyn. *The Rainbow Effect: Interracial Families.* New York: Franklin Watts, 1987.

Gecas, Viktor. "The Influence of Social Class on Socialization." In *Contemporary Theories About the Family,* edited by Wesley R. Burr, Reuben Hill, F. Ivan Nye, and Ira L. Reiss. New York: Free Press, 1979.

———. "Contexts of Socialization." In *Social Psychology: Sociological Perspectives,* edited by Morris Rosenberg and Ralph Turner. New York: Basic Books, 1981.

Gecas, Viktor, and Jeylan Mortimer. "Stability and Change in the Self-Concept from Adolescence to Adulthood." In *Self and Identity: Individual Change and Development,* edited by Terry Honess and Krysia Yardley. New York: Routledge & Kegan Paul, 1987.

Gecas, Viktor, and Michael Schwalbe. "Parental Behavior and Dimensions of Adolescent Self-Evaluation." *Journal of Marriage and the Family* 48 (1986): 37-46.

Gibbs, Jewelle Taylor. "Black Students/White Universities: Different Expectations." *Personnel and Guidance Journal* 51 (1973): 463-69.

————. "Biracial Adolescents." In *Children of Color: Psychological Interventions With Culturally Diverse Youth,* edited by Jewelle Taylor Gibbs and Larke-Nahme Huang. New York: Jossey-Bass, 1997.

Gibbs, Jewelle Taylor, and Alice Hines. "Negotiating Ethnic Identity: Issues for Black-White Biracial Adolescents." In *Racially Mixed People in America,* edited by Maria Root. Newbury Park, Calif.: Sage, 1992.

Gingrich, Newt. Letter the director of the Office of Management and Budget, 1 July 1997. Available online: http://www.projectrace.com/hot_news.html

Glenn, Norval D. "Negro Prestige Criteria: A Case Study in the Bases of Prestige." *American Journal of Sociology* 68 (1963): 645-57.

Goffman, Erving. *The Presentation of Self in Everyday Life.* New York: Anchor Press Doubleday, 1959.

Gordon, Milton M. *Assimilation in American Life: The Role of Race, Religion, and National Origin.* Oxford, U.K.: Oxford University Press, 1964.

Graham, Lawrence Otis. *Our Kind of People: Inside America's Black Upper Class.* New York: HarperPerennial, 2000.

Gunthorpe, W. "Skin Color Recognition, Preference, and Identification in Interracial Children: A Comparative Study." *Dissertation Abstracts International,* 38, no. 10-B (1978), 3468.

Gurin, Patricia, Arthur H. Miller, and Gerald Gurin. "Stratum Identification and Consciousness." *Social Psychology Quarterly* 43 (1980): 30-47.

Hall, Christine. "The Ethnic Identity of Racially Mixed People: A Study of Black-Japanese." Ph.D. diss. University of California, Los Angeles, 1980.

Hall, Ronald E. "Bias Among African Americans Regarding Skin Color: Implications for Social Work Practice." *Research on Social Work Practice* 2 (1992): 479-86.

Harris, David. "An Empirical Look at the Social Construction of Race: The Case of Mixed-Race Adolescents." Paper presented at the annual meeting of the American Sociological Association, Washington, D.C., August 2000.

Harris, David R., and Hiromi Ono. "Estimating the Extent of Intimate Contact Between the Races: The Role of Metropolitan Area Factors and Union Type in Mate Selection." Paper presented at the meetings of the Population Association of America, Los Angeles, 2000.

Harvey, Aminifu. "The Issue of Skin Color in Psychotherapy With African Americans." *Families in Society: The Journal of Contemporary Human Services* 76, no. 1 (1995): 3-10.

Hechter, Michael. "Group Formation and the Cultural Division of Labor." *American Journal of Sociology* 84, no. 2 (1978): 293-318.

Henriques, Fernando. *Children of Conflict: A Study of Interracial Sex and Marriage.* New York: Dutton, 1974.

Herring, Roger D. "Biracial Children: An Increasing Concern for Elementary and Middle School Counselors." *Elementary School Guidance and Counseling* 27, no. 2 (1992): 123-30.

———. "Developing Biracial Ethnic Identity: A Review of the Increasing Dilemma." *Journal of Multicultural Counseling and Development* 23 (1995): 29-38.

Hill, Mark. "Color Differences in the Socioeconomic Status of African American Men: Results of a Longitudinal Study." *Social Forces* 78, no. 4 (2000): 1437-60.

Hochschild, Jennifer. *Facing Up to the American Dream: Race, Class, and the Soul of the Nation.* Princeton, N.J.: Princeton University Press, 1996.

Horn, J. L., and G. Donaldson. "Cognitive Development in Adulthood." In *Constancy and Change in Human Development,* edited by Orville Brim and Jerome Kagan. Cambridge, Mass.: Harvard University Press, 1980.

Hughes, Michael, and David Demo. "Self-Perceptions of Black Americans: Self-Esteem and Personal Efficacy." *American Journal of Sociology* 95 (1989): 132-59.

Hughes, Michael, and Bradley R. Hertel. "The Significance of Color Remains: A Study of Life Chances, Mate Selection, and Ethnic Consciousness Among Black Americans." *Social Forces* 68 (1990): 1105-20.

Ichheiser, Gustav. *Appearances and Realities: Misunderstanding in Human Relations.* San Francisco: Jossey-Bass, 1970.

Johnson, Deborah J. "Developmental Pathways: Toward An Ecological Theoretical Formulation of Race Identity in Black-White Biracial Children." In *Racially Mixed People in America,* edited by Maria Root. Newbury Park, Calif.: Sage, 1992.

Johnson R. C., and C. J. Nagoshi. "The Adjustment of Offspring Within Group and Interracial/Intercultural Marriages: A Comparison of Personality Factor Scores." *Journal of Marriage and the Family* 48 (1986): 279-84.

Jones, Lisa. *Bulletproof Diva: Tales of Race, Sex, and Hair.* New York: Doubleday, 1994.

Jordan, Winthrop. *White Over Black.* Chapel Hill: University of North Carolina Press, 1968.

Kalish, Susan. "Interracial Baby Boomlet in Progress?" *Population Today* 20 (1992): 1-2, 9.

Keith, Verna, and Cedric Herring. "Skin Tone and Stratification in the Black Community." *American Journal of Sociology* 97 (1991): 760-78.

Kerwin, Christine, Joseph G. Ponterotto, Barbara L. Jackson, and Abigail Harris. "Racial Identity in Biracial Children: A Qualitiative Investigation." *Journal of Counseling Psychology* 40, no. 2 (1993): 221-31.

Kich, George. "The Developmental Process of Asserting a Biracial, Bicultural Identity." In *Racially Mixed People in America,* edited by Maria Root. Newbury Park, Calif.: Sage, 1992.

Killian, Lewis. *The Impossible Revolution, Phase II: Black Power and the American Dream,* 2d ed. New York: Random House, 1975.

King, Rebecca, and Kimberly DaCosta. "Changing Face, Changing Race: The Remaking of Race in the Japanese American and African American Communities." In *The Multiracial Experience,* edited by Maria Root. Newbury Park, Calif.: Sage, 1996.

Korgen, Kathleen Odell. *From Black to Biracial.* New York: Praeger, 1998.

Ladner, Joyce A. *Mixed Families.* New York: Anchor Press, 1977.

Lew, Jacob J. "Guidance on Aggregation and Allocation of Data on Race for Use in Civil Rights Monitoring and Enforcement." *OMB Bulletin* No. 00-02, 2000.

Lifton, Robert. *The Protean Self: Human Resilience in an Age of Fragmentation.* New York: Basic Books, 1993.

Lyles, M., A. Yancey, C. Grace, and J. Carter. "Racial Identity and Self-Esteem: Problems Peculiar to Bi-Racial Children." *Journal of the American Academy of Child Psychiatry* 24 (1985): 150-53.

Mangum, Charles Staples, Jr. *The Legal Status of the Negro in the United States.* Chapel Hill: University of North Carolina Press, 1940.

Margo, Robert A. *Race and Schooling in the South, 1880-1950.* Chicago: University of Chicago Press, 1990.

Marshall, Catherine, and Gretchen B. Rossman. *Designing Qualitative Research.* Newbury Park, Calif.: Sage. 1989.

McBride, James. *The Color of Water: A Black Man's Tribute to His White Mother.* New York: Riverhead Books, 1996.

McCracken, G. *The Long Interview* (Sage University Paper Series on Qualitative Research Methods, Vol. 13). Newbury Park, Calif.: Sage, 1988.

McGuire, William, Claire McGuire, P. Child, and T. Fujioka. "Salience of Ethnicity in the Spontaneous Self-Concept as a Function of One's Ethnic Distinctiveness in the Social Environment." *Journal of Personality and Social Psychology* 36 (1978): 511-20.

McRoy, R., and E. Freeman. "Racial Identity Issues Among Mixed-Race Children." *Social Work in Education* 8 (1986): 164-74.

Mead, George Herbert. *Mind, Self, and Society.* Chicago: University of Chicago Press, 1934.

Miller, R., and B. Miller. "Mothering the Biracial Child: Bridging the Gaps Between African-American and White Parenting Styles." *Women and Therapy* 10 (1990): 169-80.

Miller, Robin L. "The Human Ecology of Multiracial Identity." In *Racially Mixed People in America*, edited by Maria Root. Newbury Park, Calif.: Sage, 1992.

Myrdal, Gunnar. *An American Dilemma: The Negro Problem and Modern Democracy.* New York: Transaction Press, 1944.

Neal, A. M., and M. L. Wilson. "The Role of Skin Color and Feature in the Black Community: Implications for Black Women and Therapy." *Clinical Psychology Review* 9 (1989): 323-33.

Nobles, Melissa. *Shades of Citizenship: Race and the Census in Modern Politics.* Stanford, Calif.: Stanford University Press, 2000.

Omi, Michael, and Harold Winant. *Racial Formation in the United States: From the 1960s to the 1990s.* New York: Routledge & Kegan Paul, 1994.

Ortega, Suzanne, Robert Crutchfield, and William Rushing. "Race Differences in Elderly Personal Well-Being." *Research on Aging* 5 (1983): 101-18.

Park, Robert Ezra. *Race and Culture.* New York: Free Press, 1950.

Perlmann, Joel. "|'Multiracials,' Racial Classification, and American Intermarriage: The Public's Interest." Working Paper No. 195, Jerome Levy Economics Institute of Bard College, 1997.

Phinney, Jean. "Ethnic Identity in Adolescents and Adults: Review of Research." *Psychological Bulletin* 108 (1990): 499-514.

Piskacek, Vladimir, and Marlene Golub. "Children of Interracial Marriage." In *Interracial Marriage: Expectations and Reality*, edited by Irving Stuart and Lawrence Abt. New York: Grossman, 1973.

Porter, C. P. "Social Reasons for Skin Tone Preferences of Black School-Aged Children." *American Journal of Orthopsychiatry* 61 (1991): 149-54.

Porter, Judith, and Robert Washington. "Minority Identity and Self-Esteem." *Annual Review of Sociology* 19 (1993): 139-61.

Porterfield, E. *Black and White Marriages: An Ethnographic Study of Black-White Families.* Chicago: Nelson-Hall, 1978.

Poston, W. Carlos. "The Biracial Identity Development Model: A Needed Addition." *Journal of Counseling and Development* 69, no. 2 (1990): 152-55.

Poussaint, A. "Study of Interracial Children Presents Positive Picture." *Interracial Books for Children* 15 (1984): 9-10.

Ransford, Edward H. "Skin Color, Life Chances, and Anti-White Attitudes." *Social Problems* 18 (1970): 164-78.

Reuter, Edward. *The American Race Problem.* New York: Thomas V. Crowell, 1970.

Robinson, Tracy L., and Janie V. Ward. "African American Adolescents and Skin Color." *Journal of Black Psychology* 21 (1995): 256-74.

Rockquemore, Kerry Ann. "Between Black and White: Exploring the Biracial Experience." *Race and Society* 1, no. 2 (1999): 197-212.

Root, Maria. "Resolving 'Other' Status: Identity Development of Biracial Individuals." *Women and Therapy* 9 (1990): 185-205.

———. "Back to the Drawing Board: Methodological Issues in Research on Multiracial People." In *Racially Mixed People in America,* edited by Maria Root. Newbury Park, Calif.: Sage, 1992.

———. "The Multiracial Experience: Racial Borders as Significant Frontier in Race Relations." In *The Multiracial Experience: Racial Borders as the New Frontier,* edited by Maria Root. Thousand Oaks, Calif.: Sage, 1996.

Rosenberg, Morris. "The Dissonant Context and the Adolescent Self-Concept." In *Adolescence in the Life Cycle,* edited by Sigmund Dragastin and Glen Elder. New York: John Wiley, 1975.

———. *Conceiving the Self.* New York: Basic Books, 1979.

Rosenberg, Morris, and Roberta Simmons. *Black and White Self-Esteem: The Urban School Child.* Washington, D.C.: American Sociological Association, 1972.

Russel, Kathy, Midge Wilson, and Ronald Hall. *The Color Complex: The Politics of Skin Color Among African Americans.* New York: Anchor Press, 1992.

Scales-Trent, Judy. *Notes of a White Black Woman.* University Park: Pennsylvania State University Press, 1995.

Schaie, K. "The Seattle Longitudinal Study: A 21-Year Exploration of Psychometric Intelligence in Adulthood." In *Longitudinal Studies of Adult Psychological Development,* edited by K. Schaie. New York: Guilford, 1983.

Sebring, D. "Considerations in Counseling Interracial Children," *Journal of non-White Concerns in Personnel and Guidance* 13 (1985): 3-9.

Seltzer, Richard, and Robert C. Smith. "Color Differences in the Afro-American Community and the Differences They Make." *Journal of Black Studies* 21 (1991): 279-85.

Smitherman, Geneva. *Black Talk: Words and Phrases From the Hood to the Amen Corner.*Boston: Houghton Mifflin, 1994.

Sollors, Werner. *Neither Black Nor White Yet Both.* Oxford U.K.: Oxford University Press, 1997.

Sommers, V. "The Impact of Dual Cultural Membership on Identity." *Psychiatry* 27 (1964): 332-44.

Spencer, Jon Michael. *The New Colored People: The Mixed-Race Movement in America.* New York: New York University Press, 1997.

Stephan, Cookie W. "Mixed-Heritage Individuals: Ethnic Identity and Trait Characteristics." In *Racially Mixed People in America,* edited by Maria Root. Newbury Park, Calif.: Sage, 1992.

Stone, Gregory. "Appearance and the Self." In A. M. Rose (Ed.), *Human Behavior and Social Processes.* Boston: Houghton Mifflin, 1962.

Strauss, Anslem. *Mirrors and Masks: The Search for Identity.* Glencoe, Ill.: Free Press, 1959.

Suls, Jerry, and Brian Mullen. "From the Cradle to the Grave: Comparison and Self-Evaluation Across the Life-Span." In *Psychological Perspectives on the Self,* edited by Jerry Suls. Hillsdale, NJ: Lawrence Erlbaum, 1982.

Taylor, Steven J., and Robert Bogdan. *Introduction to Qualitative Research Methods: The Search for Meanings.* New York: John Wiley, 1984.

Teicher, J. "Some Observations on Identity Problems in Children of Negro-White Marriages." *Journal of Nervous and Mental Disease* 146 (1968): 249-56.

Tizard, Barbara, and Ann Phoenix. "The Identity of Mixed Parentage Adolescents." *Journal of Child Psychology and Psychiatry* 36, no. 8 (1995): 1399-1410.

U.S. Bureau of the Census. *Statistical Abstract of the United States.* Washington, D.C.: Government Printing Office, 1998.

Wardle, Francis. "Are We Sensitive to Interracial Children's Special Identity Needs?" *Young Children* 43 (1987): 53-59.

———. *Biracial Identity: An Ecological and Developmental Model.* Denver, CO: Center for the Study of Biracial Children, 1992.

Waters, Mary. *Ethnic Options: Choosing Identities in America.* Berkeley: University of California Press, 1990.

Webster, Yehudi. "Twenty-one Arguments for Abolishing Racial Classification. *The Abolitionist Examiner,* 2000. Available at: www.multiracial.com/abolitionist/word/ webster2.html

———. *Against the Multicultural Agenda: A Critical Thinking Alternative.* Westport, Conn.: Greenwood, 1997.

Weigert, Andrew J. "The Substantival Self: A Primitive Term for a Sociological Psychology." *Philosophy of the Social Sciences* 5 (1975): 43-62.

West, Candace, and Don H. Zimmerman. "Doing Gender." *Gender and Society* 1 (1987): 125-51.

Williams, Gregory. *Life on the Color Line: The True Story of a White Boy Who Discovered He Was Black.* New York: Dutton, 1995.

Williams, Kim. "Challenging Race as We Know It? The Political Location of the Multiracial Movement." In *The Politics of Multiracialism: Transforming,*

Transcending, and Challenging Racial Thinking, edited by Heather Dalmage. Albany: State University of New York Press, forthcoming.

Williams, Theresa K. "Race as Process: Reassessing the 'What Are You?' Encounters of Biracial Individuals." In *The Multiracial Experience,* edited by Maria Root. Newbury Park, Calif.: Sage, 1996.

Williamson, Joel. *New People: Miscegenation and Mulattos in the United States.* New York: Free Press, 1980.

Wintz, Cary. *Black Culture and the Harlem Renaissance.* Houston: Rice University Press, 1988.

Wright, Lawrence Wright. "One Drop of Blood." *The New Yorker,* 24 July 1994, 46-55.

Index

Affinities. *See* Group identification
African Americans:
    assimilation and, 12-13, 110, 111-112
    black power/pride, 8
    hypodescent and, 3-4, 110
    multiracial identity and, 13-15
    one-drop rule and, 110-112
    racial group membership of, ix, 10, 12
    self-hatred and, 14
    See also Black leadership; Interracial
        marriage; Phenotype
Alexander v. Holmes County Board of
    Education, 8
Anti-miscegenation, 5, 6-7, 9
Appearance, 15, 26-28
    biracial identity and, 62
    border identity and, 43-44, 92-95
    cultural meaning of, 84-85, 86, 91
    group membership and, 76-77, 80
    identity choice and, 56-57
    measurement of, 87
    mutual identification, 80-81, 90,
        94-95, 97-98, 100
    pre-view/program/review process
        and, 86, 90, 97, 98-99
    protean identity and, 96-99
    racial identity/phenotype and, 89-91
    singular identity and, 67, 95-96, 116
    skin color and, 104
    social context/phenotype and, 101-
        102
    transcendent identity and, 71-72,
        99-101

    See also Phenotype; Situated self
Appearance-identity model, 81-84, 82
    (figure), 84-86, 85 (figure)
Appiah, K. A., 114
Asante, M. K., 14
Assimilation, 11-12
    cultural vs. structural, 13
    intermarriage and, 13, 111
    minority status and, 109-110, 111-
        112
    multiracial classification and, 13-15
    structural barriers and, 12
Association of MultiEthnic Americans
    (AMEA), ix, 1

Biological classification, 2-3, 9
    miscegenation and, 5
    nonracial identity and, 51-52
    phenotypes and, 78
    racial identity, socially constructed,
        10-11, 112-113
    racial purity, 5, 13, 113
Biracial baby boom, 39
Biracial identity, viii-ix, 3, 39-40
    appearance/phenotype and, 89-91,
        103
    border identity, 41-45, 61-66, 92-95,
        115-116
    development of, 21, 42-43
    identity formation, 40-41
    multiracial classification and, 13-14
    negative treatment and, 104
    one-drop rule and, 47

About the Authors:

Kerry Ann Rockquemore received her PhD in sociology from the University of Notre Dame and is currently Assistant Professor of Sociology at Boston College. Her research focuses on parenting strategies within interracial families and the development of appropriate clinical approaches for marriage and family therapists who work with multiracial clients.

David L. Brunsma is Assistant Professor of Sociology at the University of Alabama in Huntsville. He received his PhD in sociology from the University of Notre Dame. His fields of interest include race and ethnicity, survey research, and the sociology of education. He is currently collecting data on geographic differences in racial identity formation among multiracial people.